COLLINS GEM

BASIC FACTS

SCIENCE

Edited and Revised by
D McMonagle BSc PhD

HarperCollins*Publishers*

HarperCollins Publishers
PO Box, Glasgow G4 0NB, Scotland

First published 1989
Second edition 1992

Reprint 10 9 8 7 6 5 4 3 2 1 0

© HarperCollins Publishers 1992

ISBN 0 00 459118 6 (UK edition)
0 00 459119 4 (Export edition)

Printed in Great Britain by
HarperCollins Manufacturing, Glasgow

Introduction

Collins Gem *Basic Facts* is a series of illustrated GEM dictionaries in important school subjects. This new edition has been extensively revised and updated to widen the coverage of the subject and to reflect recent changes in the way it is taught in the classroom.

Bold words in an entry identify key terms which are explained in greater detail in entries of their own; important terms which do not have separate entries are shown in *italic* and are explained in the entry in which they occur.

Other titles in the series include:

Gem *Basic Facts Mathematics*
Gem *Basic Facts Chemistry*
Gem *Basic Facts Physics*
Gem *Basic Facts Computers*
Gem *Basic Facts Biology*
Gem *Basic Facts History*
Gem *Basic Facts Geography*
Gem *Basic Facts Craft, Design & Technology*
Gem *Basic Facts Business Studies*

absorption 1. The taking in of radiated energy. When **radiation** travelling in one material meets the surface of a second, three things may happen to it.

(a) It may bounce back into the first material: this is called **reflection**.

(b) It may travel on in a new direction through the second material: this is called **refraction**.

(c) It may disappear into the second material: this is called absorption.

When a surface absorbs radiation the **energy** must appear in a new form. In most cases this is **heat** energy: the **temperature** increases.

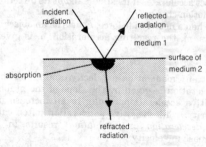

absorption

2. (of food) The process by which digested food particles pass from the **alimentary canal** into

the bloodstream. In mammals absorption takes place in the ileum, which is part of the small intestine.

acceleration (a)   The change of **velocity**, v, of an object in unit time. The **SI unit** of acceleration is the metre per second per second, m/s^2. Acceleration can be calculated using the following equation:

$$a = \frac{v - u}{t}$$

where u is the initial velocity and v is the final velocity. Acceleration is a vector quantity. An object accelerates if its **speed** and/or its direction of motion change.

When a net outside force, F, acts on an object of mass, m, the resulting acceleration, a, is given by:

$$a = F/m$$

At any moment on a velocity/time graph the acceleration is given by the slope of the graph. Positive acceleration results in an increase in velocity, while negative acceleration (often called *deceleration* or *retardation*) results in a decrease in velocity.

acid   A substance which releases **hydrogen ions** (H^+) when added to **water**. Acid solutions have a **pH** of less than 7. Common laboratory acids are:

(a) Strong acids: — nitric acid (HNO_3), **hydro-chloric** acid (HCl), **sulphuric acid** (H_2SO_4);
(b) Weak acids: — ethanoic acid (CH_3COOH), citric acid ($C_6H_8O_7$).

Strong acids ionize completely in water, weak acids only partially. A few acids are corrosive liquids and must be handled with care.
Acids:
(a) Turn blue **litmus** red.
(b) Give **carbon dioxide** when added to carbonates.
(c) Give **hydrogen** when added to certain **metals**.
(d) Neutralize **alkalis**.

acid rain   Rain polluted by acids in the atmosphere. Coal often contains substances which produce the acidic **gases** sulphur dioxide and nitrogen oxides when it is burnt. If these acidic gases are allowed to escape into the atmosphere they dissolve in any moisture present to produce acids. When the moisture falls to the earth as rain it is, in fact, acid(ic) rain.

Acid rain is responsible for considerable damage to the environment. Once soils become highly acidic, plants and animals are adversely affected and potentially harmful **ions** such as **aluminium** are able to dissolve in the acidic solution. The acidic solutions may accumulate in lakes where their effects on wildlife are devastating. Recently steps have been taken to reduce the quantity of acidic gases produced by British coal-fired power stations and car exhausts. In future it is planned to fit coal-fired power stations with flue desulphurization units to remove acidic gases before flue gases are released into the atmosphere.

air The **mixture** of **gases** which make up the **atmosphere** surrounding the **earth**. The exact composition of the air varies slightly from place to place and with height above the ground.

oxygen (20.9%)
argon (0.9%)
carbon dioxide (0.03%)
nitrogen (78.1%)

air The average composition of pure air.

Air, particularly in industrial areas, often contains pollutants. Some common examples are shown below.

Pollutant	Sources
sulphur dioxide	burning coal and oil
carbon monoxide	engines, cigarettes
nitrogen oxides	burning coal, car engines
soot	engines, fires
pollen	trees, plants
chlorofluorocarbons (CFCs)	aerosols

Air is vital for life. The **oxygen** it contains is necessary for **respiration**, and the **carbon dioxide** for **photosynthesis**. See **ozone layer**.

alimentary canal The digestive canal of an animal. In humans this canal is a tube about nine metres long running from the mouth to the anus. See **digestion**.

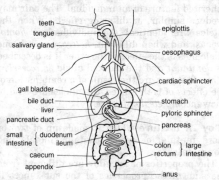

teeth
tongue
salivary gland
epiglottis
oesophagus
cardiac sphincter
gall bladder
bile duct
liver
pancreatic duct
small intestine { duodenum
                  ileum
caecum
appendix
stomach
pyloric sphincter
pancreas
colon } large
rectum } intestine
anus

alimentary canal Diagram showing the canal and digestive organs.

alkali A **base** which is soluble in **water**. Alkalis are usually **metal** hydroxides, e.g. sodium hydroxide. **Ammonia** solution is also an alkali. Alkalis are corrosive and should be handled with care. Typical properties of alkalis are:

(a) They turn red **litmus** blue;

(b) They neutralize **acids**;

(c) They have a **pH** of more than 7;

(d) They react with acids to produce a **salt** and **water** only.

allele   One of a pair of **genes** responsible for an inherited feature of an individual. The pair may produce similar, or differing effects. When the alleles are identical the individual is *homozygous*, and when different, *heterozygous*. If one allele masks the effect of the other it is described as *dominant* and the masked allele as *recessive*. When features are the result of a combination of the effects of both alleles, the alleles are said to show *incomplete dominance*.

alloy   A **mixture** which is made up of two or more **metals**, or which contains metals and **nonmetals**.

The properties of an alloy are different from the sum of the properties of the substances it contains. Alloys are used much more than pure metals. This is because an alloy can be made with a particular set of properties by bringing two or more **elements** together in the right proportions. **Aluminium** is a soft metal, but mixing it with a small amount of **copper** produces the alloy *duralumin* which is strong enough to be used in aircraft frames. Here are some other examples of alloys in common use.

Alloy	Elements it contains
brass	copper and zinc
bronze	copper and tin
pewter	**lead**, tin and small amounts of antimony
solder	lead and tin
steel	**iron** and **carbon**

alpha particle (α) This consists of two **neutrons** and two **protons** bonded together and thus it carries a positive **charge**. It contains the same particles as the **nucleus** of a helium-4 atom. Many **radioactive** nuclei give off alpha particles when they decay. An example is the common **isotope** of uranium,

$$^{238}_{92}U \rightarrow ^{234}_{90}Th + ^{4}_{2}\alpha + \text{energy}$$

The flow of alpha particles from a radioactive source is called alpha **radiation**. The energy transferred appears as the **kinetic energy** of the alpha particles. Subsequently, alpha particles collide with other particles and slow down: there is energy transfer to the substance giving a small temperature rise. As alpha radiation loses energy in matter, it causes ions to appear, hence it is an **ionizing radiation**.

Matter slows down alpha radiation very quickly. It has a range of only a few centimetres in air and cannot pass through even thin card.

alternating current (AC) A **current** which flows alternately in one direction, then in the opposite direction, around a circuit.

The **frequency** of the alternating current mains supply in the United Kingdom is 50 Hz (cycles per second). See **rectifier, direct current**.

aluminium The most abundant **metal** in the earth's crust. Aluminium has **valency** 3 and is very reactive. It is obtained by the **electrolysis** of a molten mixture of aluminium oxide, dissolved in another mineral called cryolite, using graphite **electrodes**.

Aluminium and its **alloys** are resistant to corrosion because of a protective layer of oxide which forms on the surface of the metal. (This protective layer can be thickened by a process called *anodizing*.)

amino acids *Organic compounds* which are sub-units of **proteins**. About seventy different amino acids are known but only twenty to twenty-four are found in living organisms.

Amino acids are bonded together in chains known as *peptides*. The link between adjacent amino acids is called a peptide bond or link.

When many amino acids are joined together in this way the whole complex is called a *polypeptide* and this is the basis of **protein** structure.

amino acids Structure.

amino acids A peptide bond.

ammonia A colourless **gas** with an unpleasant odour. It is very soluble in water and gives an alkaline solution (see **alkali**) which is sometimes called ammonium hydroxide. Ammonia is a **covalent compound**. It has a characteristic reaction with the gas hydrogen chloride, producing dense white fumes of ammonium chloride.

$$NH_3(g) + HCl(g) \rightarrow NH_4Cl(s)$$

Most ammonia is made by the *Haber process*. *Nitrogen* and **hydrogen** in the ratio of 1:3 react at 500°C and 20 MPa pressure on an iron **catalyst**.

$$N_2(g) + 3H_2(g) \rightleftharpoons 2NH_3(g)$$

Ammonia is produced by **bacteria** found on the roots of *leguminous* plants like peas and beans. Also, when **proteins** decompose, ammonia is released. Both of these are important sources of plant nutrients (see **nitrogen cycle**).

anemometer A device for measuring the **speed** of the wind. It is often in the form of three or four cups arranged at the ends of evenly spaced arms, attached to a spindle. The wind blowing on the cups causes the arms to rotate which, in turn, rotate the spindle. The speed of the wind is calculated from the rate of rotation.

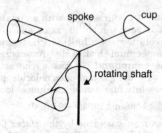

anemometer A typical design.

anhydrous Containing no **water**. The term is usually used to describe **salts** with no *water of crystallization*. For example:

	Anhydrous salt	Hydrated salt
Copper(II) sulphate	$CuSO_4$	$CuSO_4.5H_2O$
Sodium carbonate	Na_2CO_3	$Na_2CO_3.10H_2O$

The term may also be used to describe **liquids** which are perfectly dry and contain no water, e.g. anhydrous ether.

antibiotics Substances formed by certain **bacteria** and fungi which inhibit the growth of other microorganisms. Common examples are penicillin and streptomycin. Many are now made synthetically.

antibodies **Proteins** produced by the **tissues** of vertebrates in response to **antigens**. Antibodies react with antigens to make them harmless.

antigens   antibodies   antigens neutralized

antibodies Antigens are deactivated by antibodies.

antigens Materials which are foreign to an

organism. Such materials include micro-organisms such as **bacteria**, and their toxins, or transplanted **organs** or **tissue**. See **antibodies**.

artery A **blood** vessel which transports blood away from the **heart** to the **tissues**. In mammals, arteries (except for the pulmonary artery) carry bright red oxygenated blood. They divide into smaller vessels called *arterioles* which themselves eventually sub-divide into **capillaries**. Arteries have thick, elastic, muscular walls as they need to withstand the high **pressure** caused by the **heartbeat**. Compare **vein**.

thick wall — elastic muscle tissue

artery Section through an artery.

asexual reproduction Reproduction in which new organisms are formed from a single parent. Asexual reproduction does not involve the production of **gametes**. The offspring are genetically identical to each other and to the parent organism. They are sometimes referred to as clones. See **vegetative reproduction**.

assimilation The process by which food that has already been digested is incorporated into or stored in the cells of the organism. Amino acids, for example, are built up into **protein**, which is used for cell growth or maintenance. In mammals, any **glucose** which is not required immediately to provide energy in tissue **respiration** is converted in **liver** and **muscle** cells to **glycogen**. This short-term energy store can be reconverted to glucose if the blood glucose level falls (see **insulin**). Excess glucose not stored as glycogen is converted into **fat** and stored in fat storage cells beneath the skin. Fat is a long-term energy store. Excess amino acids cannot be stored and are broken down in the liver.

atmosphere 1. A unit of **pressure** equal to

atmosphere Earth's atmosphere is divided into zones.

101 325 **pascals**. Atmospheric pressure is the result of the **weight** of air pushing downwards. It varies from place to place and time to time but is always about 1 atmosphere near sea level. Atmospheric pressure decreases as height above the ground increases. See **barometer**.

2. The **mixture** of **gases** which surrounds a planet. The atmosphere on earth is **air**. The earth's atmosphere is often divided into several regions or zones. (see diagram on page 13). See also **greenhouse effect**, **ozone layer**.

atom   The smallest particle of an **element** that can exist. Atoms are the building blocks of which everything is made. They are made up of even smaller *subatomic particles*.

Subatomic particle	Position in atom	Electric charge	Relative mass
Proton	at the centre in the **nucleus**	positive	1
Neutron		neutral	1
Electron	moving around the nucleus	negative	1/1840

The proton and electron carry equal but opposite charges. The atom as a whole is neutral, hence the number of protons always equals the number of electrons. All atoms of the same element have the same number of protons and hence the same **atomic number**, but atoms of the same element may have different numbers of neutrons. See **isotopes**.

Atoms are the smallest part of an element that can take part in a chemical reaction.

atom An atom of carbon.

atomic number (Z) The number of **protons** in the **nucleus** of an **atom**. All atoms of the same **element** have the same atomic number. An atom contains the same number of **electrons** as protons, so the number of electrons also equals the atomic number.

backbone See **vertebral column**.

background radiation The radiation, from natural sources, which is always present in the earth's atmosphere. Radioactive matter exists in almost all of the rocks of the earth's crust. As it **decays** it gives off **radiation**. *Cosmic radiation* is also continually hitting the earth from space.

As a result of the above two processes a radiation detector, such as a *Geiger-Müller tube*, gives a count of about one radiation a second. Background radiation has to be taken into account when measuring the activity of other radioactive sources. The activities on earth which produce radiation, such as nuclear weapons, nuclear power stations and the medical applications of radioactive **isotopes**, appear to have little if any effect on the amount of background radiation.

bacteria   Organisms consisting of only one cell of diameter 1–2 microns. Some bacteria are harmful because they cause diseases such as *tetanus*. Some bacteria are useful, for example, as sources of **antibiotics**.

bacteria   (a) Generalized structure of a bacterium. (b) Bacterial shapes.

balanced diet A diet which contains the correct nutritional components needed for the organism to remain healthy. The term is usually used in connection with humans and domestic animals. A balanced diet for humans should contain the following:

(a) **Protein**
(b) **Carbohydrate**
(c) **Fat**
(d) **Roughage**
(e) **Vitamins**
(f) **Water**
(g) **Mineral salts**

The amounts of carbohydrate and fat should be just enough to supply the body with its energy requirements. Excess carbohydrates and fats are undesirable as they increase the amount of fat stored in the body.

barometer A device used to measure atmospheric **pressure**. In a liquid barometer, atmospheric pressure is balanced against the pressure exerted by a column of liquid. The liquid is usually **mercury**. Its high **density** means that the pressure required to balance atmospheric pressure can be attained using a relatively short column. 'Normal' atmospheric pressure is balanced by a column of mercury 760 mm high. (See **atmosphere**.)

Although the column required is relatively short, compared with those of other less dense liquids, mercury barometers are bulky and difficult to use. Also, mercury is expensive and poisonous.

barometer   Fortin mercury barometer.

An aneroid barometer operates on a different principal. It contains a partially evacuated cylindrical box. As atmospheric pressure varies it causes very small changes in the volume of the box. These changes are magnified by a system of levers and move a pointer.

Aneroid barometers are not as accurate as mercury barometers but are cheap to make and easy to use. Changes in atmospheric pressure often give some indication of forthcoming **weather** and this is sometimes shown on the barometer dial.

barometer Aneroid barometer movement.

base A substance which reacts with an **acid** to form a **salt** and **water** only. Bases are usually *metal oxides* or *hydroxides*, e.g. sodium hydroxide (NaOH), copper(II) oxide (CuO). Metal oxides and hydroxides which are soluble in water are known as **alkalis**. These are usually compounds of **group** I or II **metals**.

battery A group of two or more single electric **cells** connected together in series. A car battery consists of six 2 V cells giving a total voltage of 12 V.

bell A device constructed to make a ringing sound. An electric bell is a device based on an **electromagnet**.

When the switch is closed the circuit is completed. The iron core becomes a magnet and attracts the soft iron armature. As the armature moves across, striking the bell on the left, the circuit is broken. The spring returns the armature to its original position causing it to strike the bell on the right. This cycle is continually repeated so long as the switch is closed. Buzzers work on a similar principle.

bell

beta particle (β) A high-speed **electron** which carries negative **charge**. It is emitted by a **nucleus** during radioactive decay or nuclear **fission**. The energy transferred appears as the **kinetic energy** of the beta particle. A flow of beta particles from a radioactive source is called beta **radiation**. Beta radiation causes ions to appear when it hits matter, hence it is an **ionizing radiation**. Beta radiation travels further into matter than alpha radiation (see **alpha**

articles) but not as far as **gamma radiation**. It
is completely absorbed by a few millimetres of
aluminium.

bile A green alkaline fluid which is produced in
the **liver** of mammals. Bile is stored in the gall
bladder and passes into the duodenum through
the bile duct. In the duodenum it causes fats to be
broken into tiny droplets prior to **digestion**. This
process is called *emulsification* and it speeds up
fat digestion.

bimetallic strip A device made of strips of two
different **metals** (hence bimetallic) fixed
together. For a given **temperature** change one
metal expands (see **expansion**) more than the
other. This causes the bimetallic strip to bend.
The amount which it bends depends on the size of
the temperature change.

Bimetallic strips are used in simple **thermometers** and **thermostats**.

bimetallic strip One type used in a
simple fire alarm.

When the temperature reaches a certain value, determined by the setting of the screw, the bimetallic strip bends sufficiently to complete the **circuit** and a bell starts to ring (see diagram).

biodegradable   Capable of being broken down by biological action. This action usually involves **bacteria** and **fungi**. Biodegradable waste products are usually easy to dispose of and are not a source of **pollution**. Nonbiodegradable materials, such as plastics, are not broken down by the action of bacteria and fungi. They are difficult to dispose of and are often a source of pollution.

biosphere   The parts of the **earth** and the **atmosphere** collectively which are inhabited by living things. Living things are found:
(a) In the atmosphere immediately above the earth;
(b) On the surface of the earth;
(c) Within the surface of the earth;
(d) In lakes, rivers and oceans.
Many scientists believe that the proper functioning of the biosphere is under threat from **pollution**.

birth   The human baby is born as a result of muscular contractions of the **uterus** wall. The amniotic fluid escapes and the baby is pushed through the cervix and vagina, thus leaving the mother's body.

After the baby is born the umbilical cord, which attached it to the **placenta**, is cut. The placenta and the remaining part of the umbilical cord are then expelled from the uterus as afterbirth. The part of the umbilical cord attached to the baby will drop off within a few days. After birth the baby must use its own **lungs** for **gas exchange** and rely on its own digestive system for food. See **fertilization**, **pregnancy**.

bistable circuit (flip-flop) A **circuit** which has two stable states and may be switched from one to the other. In simple terms, an ordinary lighting circuit could be said to be a bistable circuit since it has two states: off and on. However, the term bistable is usually used to describe a switching circuit with two outputs.

bistable circuit A bistable multivibrator switching circuit using two **transistors**.

bitumen A black tarry **mixture** of high **boiling point hydrocarbons** which is left behind in the distillation of **petroleum**. It is impermeable to water and is widely used for roofing and, mixed with sand, for road surfacing.

blast furnace A furnace which allows the continuous production of molten **iron**. The furnace is charged with a mixture of coke, iron ore and limestone. At the bottom of the furnace coke and **air** (**oxygen**) react to produce **carbon dioxide**. This is an **exothermic reaction** and the **temperature** rises to 1800°C.

$$C(s) + O_2(g) \rightarrow CO_2(g)$$

More coke then reacts with the carbon dioxide to produce carbon monoxide.

$$C(s) + CO_2(g) \rightarrow 2CO(g)$$

The carbon monoxide reduces the iron oxides to iron. For example:

$$Fe_2O_3(s) + 3CO(g) \rightarrow 3CO_2(g) + Fe(l)$$

The molten iron flows to the bottom of the furnace where it is tapped off.

The limestone in the charge is decomposed by the **heat**, producing calcium oxide and carbon dioxide. The calcium oxide reacts with impurities from the iron ore (mainly silica SiO_2) and forms a molten slag.

$$CaO(s) + SiO_2(s) \rightarrow CaSiO_3(l)$$

new (limestone, ore and coke) fuel

waste gas (N_2 + CO) is burnt to heat the incoming air)

limestone coke and iron ore

steel and brick lining

hot air

slag

molten iron

blast furnace

The slag also sinks to the bottom of the furnace where it floats on the molten iron.

The iron produced by a blast furnace contains about 3% carbon and is very brittle. In **steel-making** the amount of carbon and other impurities is reduced by blowing oxygen into the molten iron.

blood A fluid **tissue** which is found in many

animals. The principal function of blood is to transport substances from one part of the body to another. The blood of mammals consists of a watery solution called **plasma** in which there are three types of **cells**: *platelets*, **red blood cells** and **white blood cells**.

The main functions of the blood in humans are:

(a) Transport of **oxygen** from the **lungs** to the tissues.

(b) Transport of **carbon dioxide** from the tissues to the lungs.

(c) Transport of toxic by-products to the **organs** of **excretion**.

(d) Transport of **hormones** from **endocrine glands** to target organs.

(e) Transport of digested food from the ileum to the tissues.

(f) Prevention of infection by:
   (i) **blood clotting**;
   (ii) *phagocytosis* by white blood cells;
   (iii) **antibody** production.

blood clotting   A thickening of the blood which occurs when blood is exposed to the **air** as a result of injury. The blood platelets produce an **enzyme** (thrombin) which causes the conversion of soluble plasma protein (fibrinogen) into fibrin. The fibrin forms a meshwork of fibres into which platelets become lodged. The resulting clot plugs the wound, restricting blood loss and the entry of microorganisms.

blood clotting

boiling point The **temperature** at which a **liquid** boils to become a **gas**. It is not fixed but depends on atmospheric **pressure**. The higher the atmospheric pressure, the higher the boiling point. Impurities in the liquid also cause the boiling point to rise. The **energy** needed to change a liquid at its boiling point into a gas is called **latent heat**.

bond The chemical link which holds **atoms** together in **molecules** and **giant structures**. Bonds are formed between atoms and are generated by **electrons**. Some atoms lose or gain electrons, forming **ions**, giving rise to **ionic bonds**. Other atoms share pairs of electrons, giving rise to **covalent bonds**.

bone The **tissue** of which the vertebrate **skeleton** is made. It contains the **protein** *collagen* which gives tensile strength, and calcium phosphate which gives bone its hardness. Some bones have a hollow cavity containing *bone marrow*. New **red blood cells** are made in the bone marrow.

brain A large mass of nerve **cells** in animals whose function is to coordinate the processes of the body. In vertebrates the brain is found at the head of the body. It is protected by the cranium and connected to the body by the spinal nerves in the **spinal cord** and by cranial nerves such as the optic nerve and the auditory nerve.

Within the human brain there are millions of nerve cells which are continually receiving and

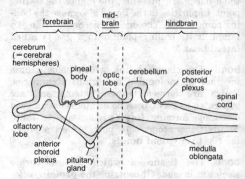

brain A generalized scheme of the vertebrate brain.

sending out *nerve impulses*. The brain is able to interpret these electrical impulses in such a way that environmental **stimuli** such as **light** and **sound** are appreciated. This allows the recipient of the stimuli to respond and adapt to the **environment** as appropriate to the situation.

The brain also coordinates all body activity to ensure efficient operation. It stores information (memory) so that behaviour can be modified as the result of past experience.

breathing (in mammals) The process of inhaling and exhaling **air** for the purpose of **gas exchange**. In mammals the gas exchange surface is situated in the **lungs**.

The exchange of air in the lungs (ventilation) is caused by changes in the **volume** of the

breathing Lungs and associated structures.

thorax. This change in volume is achieved by the action of the diaphragm and the **muscles** between the ribs (inter-costal muscles).

When the diaphragm contracts it depresses, and this increases the volume of the thorax. The air pressure outside the lungs (atmospheric pressure) is now greater than the air pressure inside, hence air is forced into the lungs. When the diaphragm is relaxed it reduces the volume of the thorax. Air pressure in the lungs is now greater than outside, and air is forced out of the lungs.

The action of the diaphragm is accompanied by

breathing The action of the diaphragm.

the raising and lowering of the rib cage to accommodate the changes in the volume of the lungs. These rib cage movements are the result of contraction and relaxation of the intercostal muscles.

The rate of lung ventilation is called the *breathing rate*. The breathing rate in humans is controlled by a part of the **brain** called the medulla oblongata (see **heartbeat**). Increased activity causes an increase in the breathing rate.

calcium A soft grey metallic **element** from **group** II of the **periodic table**. It is a fairly reactive **metal** and produces a steady stream of **hydrogen** when added to cold water. Calcium compounds are found in many common rocks such as limestone and chalk ($CaCO_3$).

Calcium metal is obtained by the **electrolysis** of molten calcium chloride.

Calcium is essential to the health of plants and animals. Calcium compounds are used by plants in building **cell** walls and in animals for building **bones**, and **teeth** (see **mineral salts**).

Calcium compounds figure prominently in our everyday lives.

(a) *Calcium carbonate* ($CaCO_3$). As limestone this is an important building stone and is used in the production of cement. Lime (calcium oxide) is produced when calcium carbonate is heated in a kiln. Limestone is also used in the production of steel.

(b) *Calcium chloride* ($CaCl_2$). **Anhydrous** calcium chloride is used as a drying agent.

(c) *Calcium hydrogencarbonate* ($Ca(HCO_3)_2$). This chemical is responsible for temporary **hardness of water**.

(d) *Calcium hydroxide* ($Ca(OH)_2$). This is slaked lime, made by adding lime to water. The resulting limewater is used in the production of mortar.

(e) *Calcium oxide* (CaO). This is lime. It is used in agriculture to combat excessive acidity in **soils**.

(f) *Calcium sulphate* ($CaSO_4$). The chemical responsible for permanent hardness in water.

camera   An optical instrument with which it is possible to produce a permanent representation of a scene. **Light** from the scene is focused on, and absorbed by, emulsion on a film. It causes chemical changes at each spot on the emulsion. The nature of the changes depend on the colour and brightness of the light. Processing the film makes the picture permanent. The operation of the camera is as follows:

(1) The distance between the **lens** (a) and the film (d) is set so that the image is sharply focused on the film.

(2) The *iris diaphragm* (b) is put to a setting (aperture) which lets the right amount of

light through.
(3) The shutter (c) opens, allowing the film to be exposed to the light for the right length of time.
(4) All of the parts of the camera are contained in a light-tight box which is called the camera body (e).
(5) The inside of the camera is painted matt black to prevent any light being reflected within it.

camera   The working parts of a camera.

capillaries   The smallest blood vessels, formed from arterioles and eventually draining into venules and then **veins**. Capillaries form a net-

capillaries   (a) Section through a capillary. (b) Capillaries and tissues.

work within vertebrate **tissue**. The capillary walls are only one **cell** thick and allow the **diffusion** of substances between the blood and the tissues via a liquid called tissue fluid (*lymph*).

carbohydrates These are *organic compounds* which contain the elements **carbon** (C), **hydrogen** (H) and **oxygen** (O) and have the general formula $(CH_2O)_n$.

Carbohydrates are found either as single **sugar** units or as chains of two or more sugar units bonded together. There are three main groups of carbohydrates; *monosaccharides*, *disaccharides* and *polysaccharides*. Simple carbohydrates, particularly **glucose**, are the **energy** source within living **cells**. 1 g of carbohydrate contains 17.1 kJ of energy.

Long-chain carbohydrates form some structural parts of cells, for example, **cellulose** in plant cell walls. They also act as food reserves, for example, **glycogen** in animals and **starch** in plants.

carbon A nonmetallic **element** which is in **group** IV of the **periodic table**. It is found in nature in two different forms or *allotropes*; diamond and graphite. All living tissue contains carbon compounds (*organic compounds*), e.g. **carbohydrates**, **proteins**, **fats**, and life would not be possible without these.

Carbon burns in **air** or **oxygen** to produce **heat** and **light energy**. Coke, **coal** and charcoal are all impure forms of carbon. They are often used as **fuels**.

carbon cycle The circulation of the **element carbon** and its **compounds** in nature. Most of this cycle is the result of the metabolic processes of living organisms.

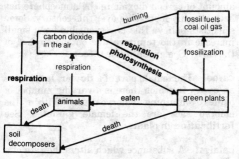

carbon cycle A summary of the cycle.

carbon dioxide A gas which makes up 0.03% of **air**. It is formed by a variety of processes.

(a) By the **combustion** of **carbon** in a plentiful supply of **air** or **oxygen**. (Combustion in a limited supply of air will also produce the

poisonous gas carbon monoxide).
(b) During the **fermentation** of **sugars**.
(c) As a waste product of **respiration**.
(d) By the action of **heat** (in most cases) or **acids** on *carbonates* in the laboratory.

Carbon dioxide plays a vital role in both **photosynthesis** and the **carbon cycle**.

Carbon dioxide turns limewater milky or it turns a bicarbonate indicator yellow. The amount of carbon dioxide in the atmosphere has been steadily increasing over this century. Some scientists believe this is responsible for a small increase in the **temperature** on the surface of the earth. See **greenhouse effect**.

carpel The female part of a **flower**. It contains an **ovary** in which there is a varying number of ovules containing embryo sacs. Within the embryo sacs are the female **gametes**. See **fertilization** in plants.

catalyst A substance which alters the rate of a chemical reaction either speeding it up or slowing it down. The catalyst remains unused at the end of the reaction. The process is called *catalysis*. The transition metals or their **compounds** are often useful catalysts. Some examples are shown below.

Almost all of the chemical reactions which go on inside animals and plants are controlled by catalysts. These organic catalysts are called **enzymes**.

Catalyst	Process
iron	hydrogen + nitrogen → **ammonia** (Haber process)
vanadium (V) oxide	sulphur dioxide + oxygen → sulphur trioxide (contact process) for making **sulphuric acid**
platinum/rhodium **alloy**	ammonia → nitric acid

cell 1. A unit of cytoplasm controlled by a single **nucleus** and surrounded by a selectively permeable membrane. Cells are the basic units of which most living things are made.

cell wall ——

chloroplasts —
vacuole —

(a)   *plant cell*

— cell membrane —
— nucleus
— cytoplasm

(b)   *animal cell*

cell The structures of (a) a plant cell and (b) an animal cell, showing some similarities and differences.

2. A device which provides a transfer to electrical **energy**. For example, a dry cell (commonly but incorrectly called a **battery**) such as might be used in a torch, gives electricity as the chemi-

cal potential energy is transferred to electrical energy.

A *photoelectric* cell provides transfer from light to electric energy. Some calculators and watches are fitted with this type of cell.

cell   A 1.5 volt dry cell.

cellulose   A **carbohydrate** which forms the framework and gives strength to plant **cell** walls. Humans are unable to digest cellulose; however, it has an important role as **roughage**. In mammals which are herbivores, populations of **bacteria** are present in the caecum and appendix. They produce an **enzyme** called *cellulase* which digests cellulose into **glucose**.

cement   A substance which is used to bind other substances together. Portland cement is widely used in building work. It is made by heating a mixture of limestone and clay to about 1700 °C. The product is ground with gypsum. Cement is mainly composed of calcium silicates and aluminates. When cement powder is mixed with water it undergoes a **chemical change** and sets hard. *Concrete* is formed when cement is mixed with sand or gravel (often called aggregate) and water. The strength of the concrete is determined by the proportion of cement in the mixture.

centripetal force   A centre-seeking force. An object is said to be in equilibrium either when it is at rest, or moving at constant speed in a straight line. It cannot accelerate unless a net outside **force** acts on it. To make an object follow a curve a force must act on it towards the centre of the curve. This is a centripetal or centre-seeking force. When an object is whirled in a circle on the end of a length of string the object is pulled towards the centre of the circle by tension in the string. This tension provides the centripetal

centripetal force

force. If the string breaks the object flies off in a straight line.

The centripetal force which keeps objects in **orbit** around the earth is provided by **gravity**.

ceramics Materials made from inorganic chemicals (see **inorganic chemistry**) by high temperature processes. Ceramics are resistant to chemical attack and range from semiconductors to electrical insulators. A wide range of materials may be described as ceramics including abrasives, **cement** and cement products, glass and pottery.

chain reaction A situation where one event causes a second which, in turn, causes a third, and so on. An important chain reaction is the one

chain reaction The chain reaction which occurs in a nuclear power station.

which occurs in a **nuclear power** station. When the **nucleus** of an **atom** of **uranium**-235 absorbs a **neutron** it undergoes nuclear **fission**. This produces two smaller nuclei, **energy** and three more neutrons. The three neutrons can, in turn, hit the nuclei of three more atoms of uranium-235 producing nine neutrons and so on.

charge A property of some subatomic particles. Two types of charge exist and they have the names *positive* (as on the **proton**) and *negative* (as on the **electron**).

Opposite charges attract each other while like charges repel each other. Normal **atoms** have equal numbers of protons and electrons; they are neutral and have no net charge. When electrons are gained or lost by atoms charged **ions** are produced.

Charge in motion is called **current** and involves **energy** transfer. The unit of charge is the *coulomb* (C). This is the total charge carried by about 1.6×10^{19} electrons — it is the charge transferred by one ampere in one second.

chemical change A change in which one or more chemical substances are changed into different substances by the breaking and making of chemical **bonds** between the **atoms**. Chemical change is usually accompanied by the giving out or taking in of **heat energy**. See **exothermic**

reaction, endothermic reaction. Compare **physical change**.

chlorine (Cl_2) The second of the **halogen (group** VII) **elements**. It is a green **gas** at room **temperature** and is very reactive. It is very unpleasant if breathed in: it attacks the **lungs** and throat and produces a choking effect. Chlorine has been used as a chemical weapon.

Chlorine occurs naturally as chlorides: sodium chloride is abundant in sea water. It is extracted by the **electrolysis** of sodium chloride solution (during the industrial production of sodium hydroxide). Chlorine is used widely in a range of applications:

(a) It is used in the manufacture of chemicals such as **polymers** (PVC), **pesticides** (DDT), disinfectants (TCP) and solvents (for dry cleaning).

(b) It is added to drinking water and to water in swimming pools in order to kill dangerous **bacteria**. The process is called chlorination.

Chlorine is a vigorous oxidizing agent which readily reacts with most elements. It is prepared in the laboratory by the **oxidation** of concentrated **hydrochloric acid**.

concentrated hydrochloric acid + potassium manganate(VII) → chlorine

Metal chlorides. These are usually **ionic com-**

pounds, e.g. sodium chloride (NaCl), barium chloride ($BaCl_2$) (see **salts**). They react with concentrated **acids** to produce hydrogen chloride gas.

$$H_2SO_4(l) + NaCl(s) \rightarrow NaHSO_4(s) + HCl(g)$$

| concentrated sulphuric acid | sodium chloride | sodium hydrogen-carbonate | hydrogen chloride |

Nonmetal chlorides. These are **covalent compounds**. They are usually either low **boiling point liquids** such as tetrachloromethane (CCl_4) or gases such as hydrogen chloride.

chlorophyll A green pigment found in the **chloroplasts** of plant **cells**. This pigment absorbs the light **energy** needed for **photosynthesis**.

chloroplasts Structures found in the cytoplasm of green plant **cells**. Chloroplasts contain the green pigment **chlorophyll** and **photosynthesis** occurs in them.

chromatography An important technique for separating **mixtures** of solutes in a solvent. The following is a simple method of separating the different dyes in a sample of ink.

(a) Place a small spot of ink onto a piece of filter paper.

(b) Stand the filter paper in a beaker containing a small amount of water. The level of water must be below the position of the ink spot. Leave the filter paper until water has risen up to the top of it.

(c) The different dyes in the ink will be carried up the filter paper by the water at different rates, hence they will be separated.

This process occurs because some substances cling to the paper more tightly than others. Chromatography has a wide range of applications including the separation of **proteins**, forensic samples, **enzymes** and **viruses**. It works with very small samples.

different dyes

position of original spot of ink

ink

water

chromatography   Method of separating different dyes in a sample of ink.

chromosomes   The hereditary material contained within the **nucleus** of a cell. The information they contain causes features of one generation to be passed on to the next. Each **species** has characteristic numbers and types of chromosomes.

In humans the *chromosome number* is 46. When a nucleus divides by *mitosis* this *diploid* number (46) of chromosomes is maintained in the new nuclei formed. When a nucleus divides by *meiosis* the new nuclei formed have only half of the diploid number of chromosomes (23) and they are called *haploid* **gametes**. Two haploid gametes join to form a diploid *zygote*.

In diploid cells the chromosomes occur in similar pairs known as *homologous pairs*. Thus a human diploid cell contains 23 pairs of *homologous chromosomes*.

Chromosomes control the activity of the cell. They are made of many subunits called **genes** which contain coded information in the form of the substance **DNA**.

circuit A number of electrical components joined by *conductors* to a source of electrical **energy**. *Circuit diagrams* show, in simple form, the order in which the components are connected. (See Appendix B for symbols used.)

Circuits (a) and (b) show two lamps connected to two cells. In circuit (a) the bulbs are connected in *series* while in circuit (b) they are connected in *parallel*.

In circuit (c) an *ammeter* is connected in series with a lamp to measure the **current** in it and a *voltmeter* is connected in parallel to measure the **voltage** across it.

circuit   (a) A series circuit. (b) A parallel circuit.

circuit   Series and parallel circuits combined.

circulatory system   Any system of vessels in animals through which fluid circulates; for example **blood** circulation and the lymphatic system.

In mammals there are two overlapping blood circulations:
(a) Circulation between the **heart** and the **lungs**.
(b) Circulation between the heart and the body.
This arrangement is called a *double circulatory system*. The heart acts as the pump for both

circulatory system The double circulatory system of mammals.

circulations and forces blood through the circulatory system always in the same direction.

classification   This is a method of arranging living organisms into groups on the basis of similarities of structure. The present system of classification was devised by Carl von Linné (Linnaeus) in the 18th century. Organisms are first sorted into large groups called *kingdoms* which are divided into smaller groups called *phyla* in animals, and *divisions* in plants. Further subdivisions occur producing subsets containing fewer and fewer organisms which have more and more common features.

Ultimately genera (singular *genus*) are divided into groups of closely related **species**. Some examples are shown in the Table.

clone   A group of organisms which are *genetically identical*. Clones are the result of **asexual reproduction**.

		clones
parent organism	→ asexual reproduction	→ identical offspring

For example, strawberry runners are clones of a single parent plant.

coal   A **fossil fuel** formed over millions of years from fossilized plant material. It has a complex

Classification

	human	dog	oak	meadow buttercup
kingdom	Animal	Animal	Plant	Plant
phylum/division	Chordata	Chordata	Spermatophyta	Spermatophyta
class	Mammalia	Mammalia	Angiospermae	Angiospermae
order	Primates	Carnivora	Fagales	Ranales
family	Hominidae	Canidae	Fagaceae	Ranunculaceae
genus	Homo	Canis	Quercus	Ranunculus
species	sapiens	familiaris	robur	acris

classification The scheme of arranging living organisms into subdivisions.

chemical structure and contains **compounds** made of **carbon**, **hydrogen**, **oxygen**, nitrogen and **sulphur**. Coal is used as a **fuel** to produce **heat** in power stations, industry and the home. The compounds containing sulphur and nitrogen produce acidic **gases** when they are burned. These gases are responsible for **acid rain**.

If coal is heated in the absence of air, coal tar is produced. Earlier in this century this was an important source of a whole range of organic chemicals such as phenol which is used in the preparation of dyes, drugs and **polymers**. Now most of these products are made from **petroleum**; however, as the world's petroleum reserves decrease, scientists are trying to find ways of converting coal into petroleum products.

About 20% of coal is used to make coke. See **resources**.

colour The name we give to our perception of different wavelengths of visible **light**. The colour of visible light varies with wavelength. The wavelength range of visible light is about 400–760 nm. This range contains several hundred *hues* (distinguishable colours) which merge into each other as we go from the deepest red to the deepest violet. The range is often divided into six or seven bands.

White light is a **mixture** of equal amounts of all the different hues. **Refraction** of a parallel

Wavelength/nm	Colour
400–420	violet
420–450	indigo
450–500	blue
500–560	green
560–600	yellow
600–650	orange
650–760	red

beam of white light by a prism can produce the **spectrum** of colours listed above. This is also possible by another method using **diffraction**. The process of separating white light into its constituent colours is called **dispersion**.

Red, blue and green are the three *primary colours*. A mixture of any two of these produces a secondary colour and a mixture of all three produces white light. Mixing coloured light is called *mixing by addition*.

There are few surfaces which reflect all light. Most absorb some wavelengths and reflect others. An object will appear the colour of the light which it reflects. For example, when red paint is illuminated with white light the paint will absorb all colours except red. The red is reflected, making the paint look red. An object which absorbs all colours appears black.

Most paints contain several different pigments each of which will absorb particular colours. Mixing different coloured paints does not produce the same results as mixing different coloured lights.

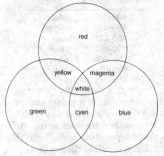

colour   Mixing by addition.

combustion   In the process of combustion (burning), substances undergo a chemical reaction with **oxygen** (often from the **air**). **Heat** and **light** are usually produced during combustion and oxidation takes place.

community   Groups of different **species** of plants and animals living and interacting together within a particular **habitat**. For example, in a small pond there may be different species of fish, amphibians, insect larvae, plants etc, living and interacting together.

compound   A pure substance which is made of

toms of two or more **elements** chemically onded together. The **properties** of compounds re quite different from the properties of the ele-nents from which they are made, e.g. sodium is a oisonous metal which reacts very violently with ater, chlorine is a poisonous gas with a choking nell, yet sodium chloride is used in cooking and essential to life. The atoms in a compound may e held together by either **ionic** or **covalent** onds: e.g. methane CH_4, water H_2O, sodium loride NaCl. See **mixture**.

omputer An electrical device which processes formation (**data**) according to a preset pro-ramme of instructions. All computers have the llowing basic structure.

computer

The *central processing unit (CPU)* controls a mathematical and logic operations. It i sometimes called the 'brain' of the computer.

The *memory* stores the programme of instruc tions (program) and the processed data.

The *clock* generates timing pulses to ensure tha all operations occur at the correct time.

The *input device* provides the CPU with the dat to be processed. The processed data is fed out t the *output device*.

concentration The concentration of a *solutio* is a measure of how much *solute* (solid) is dis solved in the solution. It is usually expressed i terms of **mass** (e.g. grams), or number o particles (e.g. **moles**) per unit **volume**. Fo example, the concentration of 1 **dm**^{3} of sodiu hydroxide solution containing 40 g of sodiu hydroxide (relative molecular mass: NaOH=4(could be written as:

$$40 \text{ g/dm}^3 \text{ (g/l) or 1 mol/dm}^3 \text{ (=1 M)}$$

conduction 1. *Electrical*. The process o transferring a **charge** through a medium. I nearly all cases there is also an **energy** transfer

Substances can be classified according to th ease with which they allow a charge to pass.

(a) A *conductor* is a substance which is able t pass charge with ease;

(b) A *semiconductor* is fairly good at passin charge;

(c) An *insulator* will only allow charge transfer when the **voltage** applied to it is very high.

Applying a voltage to a sample involves making one end of it positive with respect to the other. If the sample contains charges which are free to move they will be drawn towards the opposite charged end.

Metals and **carbon** are the only **solids** which will allow charge to pass with ease. This is because a metal contains free **electrons** which are able to move about. The applied voltage makes the electrons accelerate. As they move they collide with each other and with the positive **ions** which form the bulk of the metal. These collisions cause the electrons to slow down; they introduce **resistance** to the flow of charge. There is also energy transfer which causes **temperature** rise (see **fuse**).

The flow of charge per second is called the **current**. It depends on the voltage and on the resistance.

It is normal to give current direction as positive to negative (*conventional current*). However, when the charge carriers are electrons, the current is in fact a flow of negative charge moving from negative to positive (*actual current*).

Apart from liquid metals, other **liquids** will conduct if they contain positive and negative ions. These are compounds which are either molten or in solution and are called *electrolytes*.

In this case the flow of charge causes chemical changes; the process is called **electrolysis**. In insulators all the electrons are either firmly attached to the atomic nuclei or involved in chemical bonding; they are not free to move.

conduction Electrical conduction.

2. *Thermal.* The transfer of **energy** from particle to particle in matter. Substances differ in their ability to conduct heat. Good conductors of heat are invariably good conductors of electricity. **Metals** are good thermal conductors. They contain free moving **electrons** which carry energy rapidly from points at a high **temperature**. **Nonmetals** are very poor conductors and are used for thermal **insulation**. Compare **convection**, **radiation**.

conservation of energy The principle that the total energy in any system is constant. It is a basic law of physics that **energy** cannot be created nor destroyed. In any energy transfer, the output energy is equal to the input energy (see **efficiency**). This law was shown to be incomplete by Einstein who proved that an object's **mass** and energy are related. The relationship may be expressed by the following equation:

Energy change = mass change × speed of light²

$$E = m \times c^2$$

The energy released in both nuclear **fission** and nuclear **fusion** is the result of mass changes in atomic nuclei. The *law of conservation of mass and energy* is that the sum of an object's mass and energy is constant unless there is transfer to or from outside.

convection The transfer of **energy** through a **fluid** by movement within the fluid. An increase in the **temperature** of a fluid increases its **volume**. In turn, an increase in volume causes a decrease in **density** (since density = **mass/volume**). Thus when a fluid gets warm it rises

convection How heat is circulated through the air in a room by convection currents.

and displaces colder, more dense fluid. This sets up a convection current which circulates **heat**.

Winds and breezes are convection currents on a huge scale in the **atmosphere**.

cooling curve The general name given to a graph of **temperature** taken as a substance cools down over a period of time. The shape of the graph indicates when a change of state has taken place (see **latent heat**). It is particularly useful for finding the **melting point** of a **liquid** — the same temperature at which the liquid becomes solid. It may also be used to find the heat or temperature losses due to cooling.

copper A transition **metal** which plays an important part in our lives. It is a vital trace element in our bodies and we need between 1–2 mg per day.

Copper comes low down in the **electrochemical series** and is an unreactive metal. It is sometimes found as the free (native) metal which is an indication of its lack of reactivity. It does not produce **hydrogen** when added to dilute acids.

Copper is obtained from its *sulphide* ores chalcopyrite ($CuFeS_2$) and bornite (Cu_5FeS_4), and its *carbonate* ores malachite ($CuCO_3 . Cu(OH)_2$) and azurite ($2CuCO_3 . Cu(OH)_2$). The final stage of purification is achieved by **electro-**

lysis. Impure metal is used for the *anode*, pure copper for the *cathode* and copper(II) sulphate as the **electrolyte**. Copper is widely used in plumbing and for electrical wiring.

corrosion The eating away of a substance by chemical reactions with other substances. Good examples are:

(a) The weathering of limestone buildings by rainwater which contains **acids**.

(b) The rusting of **iron** and **steel** due to oxidation in the presence of **air** and moisture.

Corrosion begins on the surface and often a surface layer is formed which protects the rest of the material. In rusting this is not the case. The rusting process goes through iron and some steels until it is all corroded. See **rust**.

covalent bonds This type of **bond** is formed when two atoms come together and share **electrons**, e.g. **hydrogen atoms** have one electron each. The atoms in a **molecule** of hydrogen share both electrons between them.

Each shared pair of electrons produces a covalent bond. Covalent bonds are usually found in **compounds** which only contain nonmetallic **elements**, e.g. **carbon dioxide** (CO_2), **ammonia** (NH_3), hydrogen chloride (HCl), and elements which exist as molecules which contain two or more atoms, e.g. **hydrogen** (H_2), **oxygen** (O_2), nitrogen (N_2), **chlorine** (Cl_2). Covalent bonds which contain two electrons, i.e. one shared pair, are called single bonds. Many molecules contain *double* or *triple* bonds.

covalent bonds   A molecule of hydrogen.

ethane

ethene

$$H-C\equiv C-H$$ ethyne

covalent   bonds   Molecular   structures containing single, double and triple bonds.

covalent compounds   Compounds which contain covalent bonds. They tend to be non-conductors and have low **melting** and **boiling points**.

current (*I*)   The flow of **charge** through an electrical conductor (see **conduction, electrical**). The unit of current is the ampere, A; often abbreviated to amp. One amp is the current when a charge, Q, of one coulomb passes in one second, $I = Q/t$.

Currents in **circuits** are the basis of many electrical devices and electronic systems. In each case the effects of charge and **energy** transfer are used. Energy transfer may produce **light**, **temperature** change, magnetic effects, **chemical changes** and mechanical **force**.

data 1. Information, in the form of numbers, letters and symbols, which is accepted, processed and stored by a **computer**. See **data base**.
2. Observations and measurements obtained from an experiment, often, but not always, in the form of numbers. See **data presentation**.

data base A method of storing **data** (as a **data file**) in a **computer** in such a way that it can be accessed in many different ways for use in various applications.

data file This consists of a series of *records*. Each record is further divided into a group of *fields*. Each record has the same fields but not usually the same data in them. For example: a data file may contain the first name, surname and age of twenty people. There are twenty records corresponding to twenty people and three fields: first name, surname and age.

data presentation Methods of displaying data

obtained by experiment in a form in which patterns and trends can be easily seen. These include *bar charts*, *graphs*, *histograms*, *pictograms* and *pie charts*.

(a)   bar chart   (b)   graph

(c)   histogram   (d)   pie chart   (e)   pictogram

data presentation (a) Bar chart. (b) Graph. (c) Histogram. (d) Pictogram. (e) Pie chart.

decay In physics this word is used to describe how the size of a measure decreases with time. In **radioactivity** it describes how the activity of a substance decreases with time. See **half-life period**.

decomposition The breaking up of a **compound** into other compounds and **elements**.

Heat is sometimes used to bring this about (thermal decomposition). Some examples are:

$$2Cu(NO_3)_2(s) \rightarrow 2CuO(s) + 4NO_2(g) + O_2(g)$$
copper(II)   copper(II)   nitrogen(IV)   oxygen
nitrate   oxide   oxide

$$2HgO(s) \rightarrow 2Hg(l) + O_2(g)$$
mercury   mercury   oxygen
oxide

$$CaCO_3(s) \rightarrow CaO(s) + CO_2(g)$$
calcium   calcium   carbon
carbonate   oxide   dioxide

denitrification This process occurs in **soil** and involves the conversion of nitrates into nitrogen by denitrifying bacteria. Denitrification causes a decrease in the fertility of the soil as the nitrogen is lost to the **atmosphere**. See **nitrogen cycle**.

density The density of a substance is the **mass** of a sample divided by its **volume**. The **SI unit** is the kilogram per cubic metre kg/m³, although density is also often given in g/cm³.

$$\text{density (kg/m}^3) = \frac{\text{mass (kg)}}{\text{volume (m}^3)}$$

The density of water is 1000 kg/m³ (this is equal to 1 g/cm³).

As **solid** and **liquid** volumes change little with changes of **temperature** and **pressure** their density is fairly constant. By contrast, the density of a **gas** varies widely with temperature and pressure.

dental formula A formula which describes the number and type of **teeth** in the jaws of an adult mammal with a complete set of teeth. It is expressed by writing the number of teeth in the upper jaw on one side of the mouth over those in the lower jaw on the same side.

It is not necessary to give a formula for the whole jaw as the teeth of mammals are always symmetrical about the centre of the jaw. In humans the upper and lower jaws are also symmetrical, however this is often not the case for other mammals.

deposition The process by which agents of **erosion** drop the fragments of rock which they carry along. See **rock cycle**.

detergent A cleaning agent used in washing articles such as clothes and dishes. During washing a detergent acts in two ways:
(a) It reduces the surface tension of the water thus allowing the water to wet things more thoroughly.
(b) It brings together the water and (normally insoluble) fat, oil or grease to form an emulsion.
If the presence of a detergent is accompanied by

rapid movement, such as the washing action of a washing machine, then particles of dirt and grime are removed and the article is cleaned.

Detergents are able to form an emulsion because one part of the **molecule** is ionic and another part (the **hydrocarbon** chain) is covalent. The ionic part is attracted to water while the covalent part is attracted to oil. Thus detergent molecules hold the water and oil together.

Soaps work in a similar way to detergents; however their action is generally less vigorous. Soaps are made from natural oils and are sodium salts of long chain carboxylic acids. Detergents are made from **petroleum**.

detergent The structure of a typical detergent molecule.

dialysis A process in which small **molecules** are separated from larger ones using a *semipermeable membrane*. Only the smaller molecules are able to pass through the membrane in an excess of water. It is by this process that the

kidneys are able to purify the **blood**. The principal is also the basis for kidney machines, used to purify the blood in cases of kidney disease or failure.

diffraction The bending of a wave round the edge of an opaque object into the region of shadow. The effect of diffraction on water waves can be seen in harbours or with a ripple tank.

All waves can diffract around suitable objects. The effect is greatest when the size of the object is about the same as the wavelength of the wave.

Light diffracted by a narrow slit produces a set of interference fringes. As diffraction depends on wavelength, it can produce **dispersion**. A diffraction grating can be used to produce spectra.

diffraction

diffusion This is the way in which **fluid** particles spread from a source through the space available. For example, if a **gas** with a distinct odour (such as hydrogen sulphide) is released in the corner of a room it takes very little time before people all over the room will be able to smell it. Diffusion in **liquids** is not as fast as in gases, because the particles move at slower speeds and collide more often. Diffusion is part of the evidence for the **kinetic model** of matter.

digestion The breakdown of large insoluble food particles into small soluble particles by the action of **enzymes**. This occurs prior to **absorption** (see **absorption** 2) and **assimilation**. In many animals, including mammals, digestion and absorption take place in the **alimentary canal**. The table on page 68 gives some details of the digestive enzymes found in the human alimentary canal.

diode A two-electrode device which will allow an electric current to pass in one direction only.

The main use of diodes is as **rectifiers**. Older types of diode include diode valves and the point-contact diode ('cat's whisker').

lit bulb   unlit bulb

diode

location	glands	enzyme	substrate	product
mouth	salivary	amylase	starch	maltose
stomach	gastric	pepsin	protein	peptides
		rennin	milk protein	coagulated milk
Oduodenum	pancreas	amylase	starch	maltose
		lipase	fats	fatty acids+glycerol
		trypsin	protein+ peptides	amino acids
ileum		lactase	lactose	glucose+galactose
		lipase	fats	fatty acids+glycerol
		maltase	maltose	glucose+fructose
		peptidase	peptides	amino acids

digestion Digestive enzymes in humans.

The modern p–n junction semiconductor diode has now replaced other types for almost all applications.

direct current (DC) A flow of **charge** in one direction only. Direct current may be constant or may vary in value. See **rectifier, alternating current**.

dispersion The separating of **radiation** into bands of different wavelengths by bending it (**refraction** or **defraction**). The angle of bending depends on the wavelength. For example, *white light* consists of light rays of different wavelengths (see **colour**). When white light passes from **air** into glass, the rays bend progressively, going from the reds to the blues. The white light is dispersed.

dissociation The breaking up of a **compound** into smaller **molecules** or **ions**. This dissociation is reversible.

$$HCl(aq) \rightleftharpoons H^+(aq) + Cl^-(aq)$$
$$\underset{heat}{NH_4Cl(s)} \rightleftharpoons NH_3(g) + HCl(g)$$

dm³ The symbol for the cubic decimetre. The cubic decimetre is used by scientists to measure **volume**. In everyday life, volume is measured using another unit, the litre. One litre is exactly equal to one cubic decimetre.

$$1000 \text{ cm}^3 = 1 \text{ dm}^3 = 1 \text{ litre}$$

DNA (deoxyribonucleic acid) A major con stituent of **genes** and hence **chromosomes**.

A *polynucleotide* chain consists of a series o alternating **sugar** and phosphate groups witl *nitrogen bases* attached to the sugar groups.

where Ⓟ = phosphate group
Ⓢ = sugar group
Ⓝ = nitrogen base

DNA   A polynucleotide chain.

DNA consists of a double polynucleotide chair twisted into a helix. The two chains are hel together by bonds between nitrogen base pairs These nitrogen bases can only link as com plimentary pairs: thymine with adenine, and guanine with cytosine. The number and sequence of the base pairs in the DNA polynucleic chain represents coded information (the *genetic code*) which allows the transfer o hereditary information from generation to generation.

D.N.A. double helix (with section unwound)

Nitrogen bases
- ⊤ = Thymine
- Ⓐ = Adenine
- Ⓖ = Guanine
- Ⓒ = Cytosine
- Ⓢ = Sugar group (deoxyribose)
- Ⓟ = Phosphate group.

DNA The double helix (with section unwound).

ear The **organ** responsible for hearing and balance in vertebrates. Hearing is a sensation which is produced by vibrations or **sound waves**. These are converted into nerve impulses by the ear and transmitted to the **brain**, where they are interpreted.

The ear is often considered in terms of three sections.

(a) *Outer ear.* The pinna is the part of the ear which we can see. It is funnel-shaped and directs sound waves into the ear and along the auditory canal. At the end of the canal there is a thin membrane, the eardrum (tympanum), which is made to vibrate by the sound waves.

(b) *Middle ear.* This is an air-filled cavity. It is connected to the back of the mouth (pharynx) by the eustachian tube. This allows **air** into the middle ear so that the air **pressure** on each side of the eardrum is always the same. Within the middle ear there are three tiny **bones** called ossicles. The individual bones are named from their shape; malleus (hammer), incus (anvil) and stapes (stirrup). The ossicles transmit and amplify the vibrations of the eardrum to a membrane called the oval window which lies between the middle and the inner ear.

ear The parts of the ear.

(c) *Inner ear.* This is filled with **fluid** and contains the cochlea and semicircular canals. The vibration of the stapes against the oval window sets up waves in the fluid of the cochlea. These waves stimulate receptor cells (hair cells) which result in impulses being sent to the brain via the auditory nerve. Within the brain these impulses are interpreted as sounds.

Balance is maintained by the semicircular canals, in association with information received from the **eyes** and **muscles**. The canals contain fluid and receptor cells. The **cells** are stimulated by movement of the fluid during changes of posture. The nerve impulses initiated by these cells travel to the brain along the auditory nerve and trigger the response needed for the body to retain normal posture.

ear Sound waves are converted into nerve impulses by the ear and transmitted to the brain for interpretation.

earth 1. To join an object to earth by a conductor so that it will share any net **charge** it has with the earth. Because the earth is so large, this effectively means that the earthed object cannot

earth (a) A device earthed to a metal plate in the ground. (b) Symbol for earth.

keep charge. To earth an object it is connected to a metal plate or stake in the ground.

The green/yellow coated wire in a household cable should be connected to the earth pin of the **three-pin plug**. In the event of a fault in an appliance the earth wire protects the user. Any charge flows to earth through the wire, and not through the person who touches the appliance.

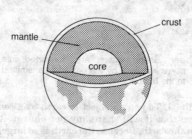

earth Structure of the earth.

2. The earth is the **planet** upon which we live. It consists of a central core surrounded by a very dense liquid mantle. Surrounding the mantle, and floating on it, is the earth's crust.

earthquake A shaking due to **energy** released by a sudden fracturing of the earth. The energy is released in the form of three types of **wave**:
(a) P-waves — push and pull, or primary waves.
(b) S-waves — shake, or secondary waves.
(c) L-waves — long waves.
The place within the earth where an earthquake starts is called the *focus*. The point on the earth's surface directly above the focus is called the *epicentre*. The magnitude of an earthquake is the amount of energy which is released. This is measured on the *Richter scale*. Earthquakes often occur at places near plate boundaries (see **tectonic theory**). Active **volcanoes** are often located in earthquake zones.

echo An effect caused by **reflection**. **Radiation** from a source appears to come, after a short delay, from somewhere else, the image. The word is most often used in connection with **sound**.

eclipse To prevent light from a source reaching an object. **Light** travels in a straight line, through a given medium, from a source to an object. A second *opaque* object, placed in such a way as to prevent light from reaching the first object, is said to eclipse, or hide, it. The two most common types are:

(a) Eclipse of the **sun** (solar eclipse). If the **moon** passes exactly between the **earth** and the sun its **shadow** passes over part of the earth's surface. People in the shadow see a solar eclipse. The eclipse is total for people in the *umbra* (full shadow) and partial for people in the *penumbra* (partial shadow).

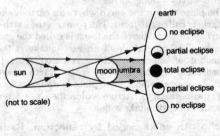

eclipse Eclipse of the sun.

(b) Eclipse of the moon (lunar eclipse). When the earth is situated in a line between the sun and the moon a lunar eclipse occurs. The moon is invisible from earth when passing through the earth's umbra and partially visible when passing through its penumbra.

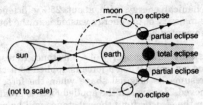

eclipse Eclipse of the moon.

ecosystem A natural unit consisting of living parts, in the form of a **community** of plants and animals; and non-living parts, in the form of a **habitat**.

habitat + community → ecosystem

Ecosystems may be forests, grasslands, lakes, rivers, etc. The driving force of all ecosystems is the energy provided by the **sun**.

efficiency The measurement of the ratio of the useful **energy** output to the total energy input in any energy transfer. It is often given as a percentage and has no units.

$$\text{efficiency} = \frac{\text{work (energy) output}}{\text{work (energy) input}} (\times 100)$$

Of course, none of the input energy is destroyed; some is simply transferred into unwanted forms, e.g. a car engine transfers chemical energy into mechanical energy with about 25% efficiency. The majority of the energy wasted is in the form of unwanted heat.

elasticity The property of a substance to resist being deformed when a force is applied to it and to resume its original shape when the force is removed. However, if the applied force is greater than the *eleastic limit* the substance will be permanently deformed and becomes a **plastic**. These effects are the result of stress/strain between the particles.

All elastic substances obey **Hooke's law**.

elasticity The stress/strain curve of a metal.

electricity **Current** electricity is a moving electric **charge** in a **circuit**. As charge moves around a circuit **energy** is transferred. This form of electricity is a convenient way of transferring energy and is widely used to power a variety of devices. (See also **static electricity**).

electricity meter A device which measures the amount of electrical **energy** used by a consumer. The unit used is the *kilowatt-hour*, kWh. (1 kWh is equal to 3.6×10^6 J). Older types of meter show the reading on a series of dials, corresponding to different powers of 10. Modern types have a single digital reading.

Domestic *electricity bills* are normally sent out to consumers every two months. They consist of a rental, for the electricity meter, and a charge for the number of units of electricity used.

electrochemical series A series in which the **elements** are arranged in order of their *standard oxidation potentials*. The following list gives some common elements in order of decreasing oxidation potential.

Potassium	2.92
Calcium	2.76
Sodium	2.71
Magnesium	2.38
Zinc	0.76
Hydrogen	0.00
Copper	−0.34
Iodine	−0.54
Bromine	−1.06
Gold	−0.80
Chlorine	−1.36
Silver	−1.42
Fluorine	−2.87

This series is useful because it allows us to compare reactivities and make predictions about whether certain reactions will or won't occur. An element will only displace less reactive elements from their **compounds**. Here are some examples:

(a) Zinc will remove the oxygen from copper oxide but copper will not remove the oxygen from zinc oxide.

(b) Hydrogen will reduce copper(II) oxide but not zinc oxide.

(c) Copper will not react with **acids** to release hydrogen. See **reactivity series**.

electrode   A conductor (see **conduction 1.**) which dips into an **electrolyte** and allows **current** to flow to and from the electrolyte. **Copper**, **carbon** and platinum are commonly used as electrodes in **electrolysis**.

During electrolysis, the electrode connected to the positive pole of the electrical supply is called the *anode* and the electrode connected to the negative pole is called the *cathode*. Chemical reactions occur at both electrodes.

electrolysis   The result obtained when a **direct** (electric) **current** is passed through a **liquid** which contains **ions** (an **electrolyte**) and **chemical changes** occur at the two **electrodes**. For example, the electrolysis of sodium chloride solution:

At the anode	At the cathode
$Cl^- \rightarrow Cl + e^-$	$H^+ + e^- \rightarrow H$
$2Cl \rightarrow Cl_2$	$2H \rightarrow H_2$
chlorine is given off	**hydrogen** is given off

This electrolysis of sodium chloride is carried out on a large scale industrially to make sodium hydroxide. Electrolysis is used to extract **metals** and **nonmetals** from their **compounds**. **Aluminium**, **sodium**, and **copper** are produced in this way, as is chlorine.

electrolysis The electrolysis of sodium chloride solution.

electrolyte An electrolyte is either:

(a) A molten **ionic compound**.

$$NaCl(l), PbBr_2(l)$$

(b) A solution which contains **ions**.

$$HCl(aq), NaOH(aq), CuSO_4(aq), NaCl(aq)$$

Chemical changes take place at the electrodes when a direct electric **current** is passed through an electrolyte. This process is called **electrolysis**. With molten compounds, such as sodium chloride, the changes are simple.

$$2Na^+Cl^-(l) \rightarrow 2Na(l) + Cl_2(g)$$

With ionic solutions the changes are more complicated. The products depend on:

(a) The **concentration** of the solution.
(b) The voltage which is applied.
(c) The type of **electrode** which is used.
(d) The nature of the ions present in the solution. The following example shows what happens when copper sulphate solution is electrolysed using different types of anode.

Anode	Reaction
(i) **carbon** or platinum	$4OH^-(aq) \rightarrow 2H_2O(l) + O_2(g) + 4e^-$
(ii) **copper**	$Cu(s) \rightarrow Cu^{2+}(aq) + 2e^-$

In process (i) oxygen is released, while in process

(ii) the copper anode dissolves. Process (ii) is used in the purification of copper.

electromagnet A device which acts as a **magnet** only when its coil is carrying an electric **current**. In the school laboratory simple electromagnets are made by winding several coils of wire around an **iron** nail and connecting the ends of the wire to a **battery**. Much larger ver-

coils of wire
iron nail

electromagnet A simple electromagnet.

cable
'core'
coil

electromagnet An industrial electromagnet.

sions, based on the same principle, are used in places like scrap yards for separating iron and **steel** from other materials.

Electromagnets are also used in a variety of electrical devices such as **bells**, **relays** and speakers.

electromagnetic induction The generation of a **voltage** across a conductor when it moves with respect to a **magnetic field**. This induced *electromotive force* (*emf*) is increased if there is an increase in:

(a) The relative motion between the conductor (usually a coil) and the magnetic field.

(b) The length of the conductor (number of coils or wire) in the magnetic field.

(c) The strength of the magnetic field.

The direction of the induced voltage is such as to oppose the change which is producing it: this is known as *Lenz's law*. Electromagnetic induction is the basis of many electrical devices such as the **generator** and the **transformer**.

electromagnetic waves A range of **radiations** which differ in wavelength but have the following properties in common.

(a) They are produced by moving electric **charge**.

(b) They travel by vibrating electric and magnetic (hence electromagnetic) fields.

(c) They move through empty space at the **speed of light** (300 000 000 m/s).

(d) They tend to be absorbed by matter in which they travel more slowly.

(e) Like all waves they show **reflection**, **refraction**, *interference* and *diffraction* effects.

(f) They are *transverse waves* and show polarization effects.

(g) They can show particle properties.

The **spectrum** of electromagnetic waves is usually divided into a number of regions. The following table shows approximate values for the wavelengths and **frequencies** of the different regions.

Region	Wavelength/m	Frequency/Hz
gamma	$- 10^{-12}$	$10^{21} -$
X-ray	$10^{-12} - 10^{-10}$	$10^{18} - 10^{21}$
ultraviolet	$10^{-10} - 10^{-7}$	$10^{15} - 10^{18}$
visible light	$10^{-7} - 10^{-6}$	$\simeq 10^{15}$
infrared	$10^{-6} - 10^{-3}$	$10^{12} - 10^{15}$
microwave	$10^{-3} - 10$	$10^{7} - 10^{12}$
radio	$10 - 10^{6}$	$10^{2} - 10^{7}$

electron A very small subatomic particle. Electrons carry a negative **charge** and move around the nuclei of an **atom**. **Ions** are formed when atoms lose or gain electrons, i.e.

gaining electrons — negative *anions*, e.g. Br^-, Cl^-, O^{2-}, S^{2-}
losing electrons — positive *cations*, e.g. Al^{3+}, Fe^{2+}, H^+, Na^+

The way in which electrons are located in an atom is called the *electronic configuration*. An electric **current** is a flow of electrons moving through a conductor.

element A pure substance which cannot be broken down into anything simpler by chemical means. There are 92 elements which occur naturally on the earth, and a small number of others have been made artificially in laboratories by nuclear reactions. All elements have a unique number of **protons** in their **atoms**.

embryo 1. A young animal developed from a zygote as a result of repeated **cell** division. During **pregnancy** in mammals, the embryo develops within the female **uterus**. When the main features of the embryo have developed it is called a **foetus**.
 2. A young flowering plant developed from a fertilized ovule. In seed plants this is enclosed within a **seed** prior to **germination**.

empirical formula The formula of a **compound** which shows the different atoms that are present in the molecule in their simplest whole number ratio. Here are some examples:

Compound	Molecular formula	Empirical formula
Ethene	C_2H_4	CH_2
Butane	C_4H_{10}	C_2H_5
Ethanoic acid	$C_2H_4O_2$	CH_2O

In many compounds the empirical and molecular formulae are the same. See **molecular formula**.

endocrine glands (or **ductless glands**). Structures found in vertebrates and some invertebrates. They release chemicals called **hormones** directly into the bloodstream. The rate at which the hormones are secreted is often a response to changes in internal body conditions; however, it may also be a response to environmental changes. The major endocrine glands in the human body are the pituitary gland (at the base of the brain), the thyroid gland (in front of the trachea), the **pancreas**, the **ovaries** (in females), the testes (in males), and the adrenal glands (above the kidneys).

endothermic reaction A reaction in which **heat energy** is taken in from the surroundings to make the reaction occur; e.g. the thermal decomposition of calcium carbonate.

$$CaCO_3(s) \rightarrow CaO(s) + CO_2(g)$$

In endothermic reactions there is more energy in the **bonds** of the products than there was in the bonds of the starting materials.

Compare **exothermic reaction**.

energy (*W*) The ability of an object to do *work*. The unit of energy is the **joule**, J. It is often useful to speak of different 'forms of energy' (although what is really meant is energy in different contexts).

(a) *Gravitational potential energy*: the work a **mass**, *m*, can do by falling a distance, *h*. $W = mgh$.

(b) *Electrical energy*: the work an electric **current**, *I*, can do in time, *t*. $W = VIt$.

(c) **Kinetic energy**; the work a mass, *m*, moving at speed, *v*, can do in coming to rest. $W = (\frac{1}{2})mv^2$.

(d) *Thermal energy*: the work needed to raise a

A gravitational potential → kinetic
B kinetic → rotation; rotation → electric
C electric → light + thermal

energy A chain of energy transfers.

mass, m, of *specific heat capacity*, c, by θ degrees. $W = mc\theta$.

In all energy transfers the useful energy output is less than the total energy input because some of the input energy will be transferred into unwanted forms. The ability of a device to transfer energy from one form to another is measured by its **efficiency**. See **conservation of energy**.

engines Systems in which the chemical (potential) **energy** of a **fuel** is transferred to mechanical energy (work). The **combustion** of the fuel in **oxygen** results in a large **volume** of hot **gas**. As the volume of gas increases it transfers energy to the system.

environment A collective name for the conditions in which organisms live. Many factors contribute to the environment including:
(a) Nonliving physical factors such as **temperature** and **light**.
(b) Living (biotic) factors such as *predators* and *competition*.
The interaction of all these factors determines the conditions within **habitats** and selects the **communities** of organisms which are best suited to the prevailing conditions. See **natural selection**.

enzymes Protein substances which act as **catalysts** within **cells**. Catalysts are substances which control the rates of chemical **reactions**. In a cell there may be hundreds of chemical reactions occurring at the same time. Each of them will require its own particular enzyme as enzymes are normally very specific in their action and will only catalyse one particular reaction. Enzymes may catalyse either:

(a) *Synthesis reactions* in which complex **compounds** are produced from simple **molecules**;

(b) *Degradation reactions* in which complex molecules are broken down into simple subunits by hydrolysis.

Enzymes work most efficiently within a narrow **temperature** range. Thus human enzymes work best around human body temperature (37 °C). Efficiency decreases above and below this temperature and at temperatures above 45 °C most enzymes are destroyed.

Enzymes work best at a particular **pH**. This varies for different enzymes.

(a) *Salivary amylase*, found in the saliva, works best at a neutral or slightly acid pH.

(b) *Pepsin*, found in the stomach, will only work in an acid pH.

(c) *Trypsin*, found in the intestine, works best in an alkaline pH.

The rate of an enzyme-catalysed reaction

equation   91

increases as the enzyme *concentration* increases.

The rate of an enzyme-catalysed reaction also increases as the concentration of the substance on which the enzyme acts increases up to a maximum point.

Most enzymes are named by adding the suffix -ase to the name of the substance the enzyme acts on. For example maltase is the enzyme which acts on maltose.

enzymes Synthesis and degradation reactions.

equation A means of expressing a chemical reaction. An equation may be in words:

hydrogen + oxygen → water

or it may be a formula (or symbol):

$$H_2 + O_2 \rightarrow H_2O$$

An equation is balanced if there are the same number of each type of **atom** on each side of the equation, e.g.

$$2H_2 + O_2 \rightarrow 2H_2O$$

is a balanced equation. There are four **hydrogen** atoms and two **oxygen** atoms on each side of it. The equation tells us that two **molecules** of hydrogen react with one molecule of oxygen to produce two molecules of **water**. Using the equation and the relative atomic masses of hydrogen (1) and oxygen (16), we can further state that 2 **moles** or 4 g of hydrogen reacts with 1 mole or 32 g of oxygen to produce 2 moles or 36 g of water.

$$2H_2 + O_2 \rightarrow 2H_2O$$
$$2(2) + 32 = 2(2 + 16) = 36$$

Sometimes *ionic equations* are used:

$$Cu^{2+} + Zn \rightarrow Cu + Zn^{2+}$$

State symbols are often added after the formula to denote which **state of matter** a substance is in, e.g. hydrogen and oxygen **gases** react to produce **liquid** water.

$$2H_2(g) + O_2(g) \rightarrow 2H_2O(l)$$

equilibrium A state of balance between opposing reactions. In a **reversible reaction** the reaction proceeds in both directions, e.g.

$$3Fe(s) + 4H_2O(g) \rightleftharpoons Fe_3O_4(s) + 4H_2(g)$$

The reactants, iron and steam, produce the products, iron oxide and **hydrogen**. As soon as the products are made they begin to react together to reform iron and steam. Eventually, a situation is reached where the rate of the forward→reaction equals the rate of the reverse←reaction. At this point the proportion of the four substances present is constant and there appears to be no reaction taking place. The forward and reverse reactions are in dynamic equilibrium.

erosion The removal of rock and mineral fragments by **water**, wind and ice. The processes of **weathering** and **erosion** operate together. Their combined effect is known as *denudation*.

erythrocyte See **red blood cell**.

ethanol One of a group of *alcohols*. It is a colourless flammable **liquid** with a **boiling point** of 78 °C. Ethanol is the alcohol in alcoholic drinks. In humans, small amounts relax the body

C_2H_5OH

ethanol

but large amounts lead to alcohol poisoning and even death.

Alcoholic drinks are made by **fermentation**. Some of the ethanol produced by industry is also made this way, however most is made by the hydration of ethene.

$$C_2H_4(g) + H_2O(l) \rightarrow C_2H_5OH(l)$$
ethene   water   ethanol

Ethanol is used in industry as a solvent and is the main constituent of methylated spirits.

evaporation The change of state from **liquid** to **gas** which can occur at any **temperature** up to the **boiling point**. At any one time, a variable population of **molecules** in a liquid will have sufficient **energy** to escape into the **atmosphere**. If a liquid is left in an open container for long enough it will all evaporate.

some molecules have enough energy to escape

molecules moving at different speeds in the liquid.

evaporation

In general, the lower the boiling point, the faster the rate of evaporation, though this also depends on the **latent heat**. Liquids which are easily turned into gases are said to be volatile.

evolution The development of complex organisms from simpler ancestors over successive generations. See **natural selection**.

excretion The process by which organisms get rid of the waste products of **metabolism**. The main excretory products are **water**, **carbon dioxide** and nitrogenous compounds such as **urea**.

   In simple organisms excretion occurs through the **cell** membrane or epidermis. In higher plants excretion occurs through the leaves. Most animals have specialized excretory **organs**. For example, in humans the **lungs** excrete water and carbon dioxide and the **kidneys** excrete urea.

exothermic reaction A reaction in which **heat energy** is released from the reactants to the surroundings. The **bonds** of the products contain less energy than the bonds of the reactants, hence the products are more stable than the reactants. Many common reactions are exothermic. All **combustion** and **neutralization** reactions are exothermic. Some important industrial pro-

cesses are also exothermic, e.g.
Haber process:

$$3H_2(g) + N_2(g) \rightleftharpoons 2NH_3(g) \text{ See ammonia.}$$

Contact process:

$$2SO_2(g) + O_2(g) \rightleftharpoons 2SO_3(g) \text{ See sulphuric acid.}$$

Compare **endothermic reaction**.

expansion The change in size of an object or material due to **temperature** change. In terms of the **kinetic model** a temperature rise causes a rise in the particles mean **energy**: i.e. the particles move more quickly and try to take up more space. This effect is greatest with **gases**. All gases expand by roughly the same amount for a given temperature change. **Solids** and **liquids** expand much less but vary greatly in the amount of expansion. See **bimetallic strip**, **water**.

Thermal expansion has many uses such as in **thermometers** and **thermostats**. It can also cause problems in structures such as clocks, roads and bridges.

eye A *sense organ* which responds to **light**. Eyes vary in complexity from the simple structures found in invertebrates to the complex eyes of insects (*compound eye*) and vertebrates.
(a) The sclerotic layer is a tough protective layer which surrounds the outside of the eye. At the

eye A vertical section through the human eye.

front of the eye it forms the transparent cornea.

(b) The choroid layer is beneath the sclerotic layer. It contains black pigmentation which prevents reflection within the eye. It is rich in blood vessels supplying the eye with food and oxygen.

(c) The retina is the inner layer of the eye. It is a layer of nerve **cells** which are sensitive to light. There are two types of cell named from their shape.

  (i) *Rods* are very sensitive to low light intensity. The eyes of nocturnal animals have high concentrations of this type of cell.

  (ii) *Cones* are sensitive to bright light and some are stimulated by light of different

light
from an
object

image
focused on
the retina

eye The lens focuses the image on the retina.

wavelengths hence they are responsible for colour vision. The *fovea* is a small area of the retina at the back of the eye which has many cones but no rods. It gives the greatest degree of detail and colour.

(d) The *blind spot* is the part of the retina where the nerve fibres, which are connected with the rods and cones, leave the eye and enter the *optic nerve*. There are no light-sensitive cells at the blind spot, hence an image here is not registered by the brain.

(e) The *aqueous humour* and *vitreous humour* are fluids contained in the eye. They help to maintain the shape of the eye, play a small part in focusing the light and allow nutrients, oxygen and wastes to diffuse (see **diffusion**) into and out of the eye cells.

(f) The *lens* is a transparent *biconvex* structure which can change curvature. It is mainly responsible for focusing light on the cells of the retina.

Accommodation is the ability of the eye to focus on objects of varying distances from it. This is possible by altering the curvature of the lens.

The lens is held in place by *suspensory ligaments* which are attached to *ciliary muscles*. When the ciliary muscles are relaxed the **pressure** of the fluid in the eye keeps the suspensory ligaments taut so the lens is pulled out and its centre is thin. This is the normal relaxed state of the eye when looking at distant objects. To look at closer objects, the ciliary muscles contract. The suspensory ligaments become slack and the lens goes fatter at its centre.

The amount of light entering the eye is controlled by the *iris*. This is the coloured part of the eye and contains muscles. The hole in the centre of the iris through which light enters is called the *pupil*. In poor light the pupils are wide open (dilated) to allow the maximum amount of light into the eye. As the light gets brighter the pupil becomes smaller (contracts). This protects the retina from possible damage. This mechanism is an example of a **reflex action**. Because the pupil is small the light rays enter the eye in such a way that they produce an image which is upside down (inverted) on the retina. This is corrected by the brain.

object   pupil   eye

eye The image is small and inverted.

Long sight and short sight are two common eye defects which can be corrected by **lenses**.

(a) A person with long sight cannot see close objects clearly because the light focuses behind the retina. This can be corrected by wearing converging (convex) lenses.

eye   Correction of long sight.

(b) A person with short sight cannot see distant objects clearly because the light focuses in

eye   Correction of short sight.

front of the retina. This can be corrected by wearing diverging (concave) lenses.

fats or **lipids** *Organic compounds* which contain the elements **carbon**, **hydrogen** and **oxygen**. Fats are made up of three *fatty acid* **molecules** (which may be the same or different) bonded to one glycerol molecule. Fat deposits under the skin act as a long-term **energy** store. 1 g of fat contains 39 kJ of energy. These deposits also provide **heat insulation**.

Fat is also an important constituent in the **cell** membrane. Its insolubility in **water** is utilized in the waterproofing systems of many organisms.

feedback A method of control in which part of the output signal is returned as the input signal.

An *amplifier* is a device in which the output signal has the same form as the input, but is greater in amplitude or size. The output/input amplitude ratio is called the *gain*. In an amplifier, feedback may be used to control the gain.

In an industrial process feedback is used to control the quality of the product. In the following example the thickness of paper is monitored by measuring the quantity of **beta particles** which passes through it.

If the number increases the paper is too thin, if it decreases the paper is too thick. This information is continually fed back to the controller which operates the rollers. This adjusts the pressure automatically in order to keep the paper at a preset thickness.

Many biochemical processes are controlled by feedback; the product of a process controls that process. For example, the thyrotrophic hormone (TSH), secreted by the pituitary gland of the **brain**, controls the amount of the **hormone** thyroxine which is produced by the thyroid gland. A high concentration of thyroxine in the body suppresses the release of TSH, thus less thyroxine is made. When the thyroxine level in the body is low, more TSH is released causing more thyroxine to be produced. Other examples of feedback in the body include control of the body water level by the antidiuretic hormone (ADH) and control of the blood sugar level by the hormone insulin. (See **kidney**.)

feedback   The thickness of paper is controlled during manufacture by feedback.

fermentation The process by which certain organisms such as **bacteria** and **yeasts** degrade organic **compounds** in the absence of **oxygen** in order to release **energy**. Fermentation is a form of anaerobic **respiration**. The following reaction shows fermentation by yeast (the basis of brewing and bread-making).

$$\underset{\underset{C_6H_{12}O_6}{\text{glucose}}}{} \xrightarrow{\text{yeast}} \underset{\underset{2C_2H_5OH}{\text{ethanol}}}{} + \underset{\underset{2CO_2}{\text{carbon dioxide}}}{} + \text{energy}$$

fertilization The fusing of haploid **gametes** during **sexual reproduction**. It results in the formation of a single cell called the *zygote* which contains the diploid number of **chromosomes**.

(a) *External fertilization.* This occurs when the gametes are passed out of the parents and fertilized, and development takes place outside the parents. External fertilization is common in aquatic organisms, such as fish and frogs, where movement of water helps the gametes to meet.

(b) *Internal fertilization.* This is particularly associated with terrestrial animals such as insects, birds and mammals. It involves the union of the gametes within the female's body. There are several advantages to internal fertilization:

(i) the **sperms** are not exposed to unfavourable dry conditions.

(ii) the chances of fertilization occurring are increased.

(iii) the fertilized **ovum** is protected within a shell (birds) or within the female body (mammals).

fertilization   Male reproductive organs.

(c) *Fertilization in humans*. During the process of copulation the penis is inserted into the vagina and sperm **cells** (produced in the

fertilization   Female reproductive organs.

testes) are passed out of the penis. The sperms move through the **uterus** and into the oviducts. If an ovum is present in an oviduct, fertilization can occur there. The fertilized ovum (zygote) continues moving down the oviduct towards the uterus, dividing repeatedly as it does so. When it arrives at the uterus the zygote, which is now a ball of cells, becomes embedded in the prepared wall of the uterus. This process is called implantation. All further development of the **embryo** occurs in the uterus. See **pregnancy**, **birth**.

d) *Fertilization in plants.* During **pollination**, **pollen** grains are deposited on the stigmas of flowering plants. The pollen grains absorb nutrients and pollen tubes grow down

male gamete moves
down pollen tube

pollen tube

ovary wall
(forms part of fruit)

embryo sac

ovule
(becomes the seed)

pollen grain sticks
to stigma

stigma

style

pollen tube enters
embryo sac
through the micropyle

male and female
gametes fuse
and fertilization occurs

fertilization   Fertilization in plants.

through the style to the ovules in the **ovary**. A pollen grain enters an ovule through a small hole called a micropyle. The bottom of each pollen tube breaks down and the male gamete enters the ovule and fuses with the female gamete. After fertilization the ovule, which contains the plant embryo, develops into a **seed** and the ovary develops into a **fruit**. See **flower**, **pollen**, **pollination**.

fertilizer A substance which is added to **soil** to increase the quantity or quality of plant growth. When crops are harvested the natural recycling of soil **mineral salts** is disturbed; i.e. mineral salts absorbed by the crops are not returned to the soil. This is called *soil depletion* and may eventually render the soil infertile. Fertilizers replenish the soil. They are often described in terms of their nitrogen, phosphorus and potassium (NPK) content. Fertilizers may be in the form of organic fertilizers, such as sewage, or inorganic fertilizers, such as ammonium sulphate. Organic fertilizers often contain trace elements: these have to be added to inorganic fertilizers.

fibre optics The transmission of information along **glass** (or Perspex) fibres as pulses of **light**. The fibre is composed of two types of glass, one contained within the other. Light enters the fibre and travels along it as a result of *total internal reflection*.

Optical fibres are very thin (less than 1 mm in diameter) and bend easily. They are far more efficient at carrying information than **copper** wires as very little **energy** is lost at each reflection. An optical fibre can carry far more information than a copper wire of similar diameter.

fibre optics   (a) Longitudinal section. (b) Transverse section.

fission This occurs when the large unstable nucleus of an **atom** splits into two smaller stable nuclei of similar size, together with other smaller particles such as **neutrons**. The total mass of the products is less than that of the starting material. The difference in mass appears as **energy**. The fission of **uranium**-235 provides the energy in a **nuclear power** station. See diagram on page 108.

fission   (n = neutron)

fixing nitrogen   Converting atmospheric nitrogen into **compounds** which are useful as **fertilizers**. Two important processes for fixing nitrogen are:

(a) The *Haber process* which converts atmospheric nitrogen into **ammonia**.

(b) The action of bacteria found on the roots of leguminous plants such as beans and peas.

See **denitrification, nitrogen cycle**.

flip-flop   See **bistable circuit**.

flower   This is the **organ** of **sexual reproduction** in flowering plants. The male part of the flower is called the **stamen** and the female part the **carpel**. Sexual reproduction relies on the transfer of **pollen** from the stamen of one flower to the carpel of the same or a different flower. See **pollination**.

fluid   This describes a **liquid** or a **gas** where the particles can flow and are not fixed in a particular position, as is the case in a **solid**. Viscosity is a measure of the reluctance of a fluid to flow. It depends upon **temperature** because the particles' 'speed' depends on temperature. A viscous liquid like syrup flows better when it is warm.

foetus The name given to a mammalian **embryo** after it develops its main features. In humans this is after about three months of **pregnancy**.

food chain A relationship involving plants and animals in which **energy** and **carbon compounds**, made by green plants via **photosynthesis**, are passed to other living organisms, i.e. plants are eaten by animals which, in turn, are eaten by other animals.

green plant	→ herbivore	→ small carnivore	→ large carnivore
(producer)	→ (primary consumer)	→ (secondary consumer)	→ (tertiary consumer)

The arrows indicate 'is eaten by'. There are many examples of food chains, e.g.

grass→ sheep→ man

Simple food chains like the one above seldom exist. More usually food chains are linked into other food chains, producing a *food web*.

All food webs are delicately balanced. If one

link should be destroyed or the numbers of a particular organism should rapidly increase or decrease, all other organisms in the web will be affected. For example, in the pond food web, if the numbers of perch started to drop due to some disease the pike population would decrease (as they would have less food) while the water scorpion population would increase (as less of them would be eaten). The larger population of water scorpions would need more food, so there would be increased pressure on the populations of tadpoles and water beetles.

food chain Part of the food web in a fresh water pond.

force (*F*) A force changes an object's motion, making it move more or less quickly and/or making it change direction. The unit of force is the newton, N; one newton is the force which will accelerate one kilogram by one metre per second per second. Newton's laws of motion relate forces to their effects and lead to the expression:

$$\text{force} = \text{mass} \times \text{acceleration} \quad (F = m \times a)$$

Here are some effects involving forces.

(a) *Gravity.* Attraction only — why objects fall to the ground when dropped.

(b) *Magnetism.* Attraction between unlike poles (N and S) and repulsion between like poles (N and N or S and S).

(c) *Electricity.* Attraction between opposite electrical charges (+ and −) and repulsion between similar charges (+ and + or − and −).

These forces act at a distance from the object they affect. Many forces act when there is, apparently, contact between particles experiencing the force. This occurs in **friction**, **weight**, push and pull (compressive and tensile) forces and in twisting. A *force meter* or *Newton meter* is sometimes used to measure force.

fossil The traces, or sometimes remains, of a plant or animal which have become embedded and preserved in rock.

fossil fuel Substances which have been formed over millions of years from the remains of animals and plants and which are used as **fuels**. Coal, **petroleum** and **natural gas** are examples of fossil fuels.

All fossil fuels are composed of compounds of the **elements carbon** and **hydrogen**. When they are burned (see **combustion**) in a plentiful supply of air they produce **carbon dioxide** and **water**. Fossil fuels also often contain small amounts of **compounds** containing **sulphur** and nitrogen which produce acidic gases when burned in air.

The world's reserves of fossil fuels are going down each year as, once used, they are not replaced by nature. Fossil fuels are nonrenewable energy **resources** (compare **renewable energy sources**). The ever-increasing amounts of fossil fuels burned around the world each year are causing some serious problems for our **environment**. See **greenhouse effect** and **acid rain**.

frequency (f)   The number of cycles of a periodic motion in unit time. For example, the number of waves passing a point in one second or the number of times a pendulum swings to and fro in one minute. The **SI unit** is the hertz, Hz.

1 hertz = 1 cycle per second

The frequency, *wavelength* and **speed** of a **wave** are related to each other by the equation:

speed = frequency × wavelength ($c = f \times \lambda$)

friction   A **force** which tends to prevent motion between two surfaces. Sometimes friction works to our advantage. For example, friction prevents our feet slipping while walking, or a car skidding when driving. Unfortunately, friction is often a disadvantage. It slows down movement and wastes **energy**, resulting in **heat** and wear.

friction Static and dynamic friction.

If a block is placed on a bench and pulled gently, as shown above, at first nothing happens:

friction (a) Even the smoothest surfaces are rough when viewed through a microscope. (b) Lubricant separates the surfaces.

the block doesn't move, thus, $P = F$. When P is gradually increased a maximum value is obtained before the block moves. This maximum value is the static or starting friction. Once the block starts to move, the value of P which is needed to keep it moving is called the dynamic or sliding friction. The dynamic friction is less than the static friction. If weights are put onto the block the value of the dynamic friction force increases in proportion. Even the smoothest surfaces are, in fact, rough when looked at with a microscope.

Frictionless motion is obviously an advantage in transport, since valuable **fuel** is used up overcoming friction. A hovercraft avoids friction with the ground by riding on a cushion of air.

fruit The ripened **ovary** of a **flower**. The **fruit** contains **seeds** formed as the result of **pollination** and **fertilization**. The fruit protects the seed and helps in its dispersal.

fruit and seed dispersal The methods by which most flowering plants spread their **seeds** far away from the parent plant. This is favourable to the plant because:
(a) It avoids competition for resources such as **water** and **light**.
(b) It ensures that the seeds will be spread over

many different **habitats**, so there is a good chance that at least some of the seeds will flourish.

Most flowering plants disperse their seeds in one of the following ways.

(a) *Wind dispersal*. Air currents carry the fruits or seeds. These are usually light and are adapted to hang in the air as long as possible.

fruit and seed dispersal Seeds adapted for wind dispersal.

(b) *Animal dispersal*. This may happen in two different ways.

   (i) Some fruits, such as burdock, have hooks which stick to the coats of animals and may be brushed off some distance from the parent plant.

  (ii) Berries such as the strawberry are succulent and are eaten by animals. The succulent part is digested but the small, hard fruits containing seeds pass through the alimentary canal of the animal undamaged. Eventually they are released in the faeces, often some distance from the parent plant.

burdock

strawberry

hooks

fruits

fruit and seed dispersal   Fruits adapted for animal dispersal.

(c) *Explosive dispersal.* Some fruits, such as sweet pea, burst open with an effect rather like an explosion. This scatters their seeds away from the parent plant. This effect is the result of unequal drying of the fruit.

Sweet pea (split open)
remains of flower   ovary wall

seeds

Wallflower (split open)

style

ovary wall

seeds

fruit and seed disposal   Fruits adapted for explosive dispersal.

fuel   A substance which releases **heat energy** when it is treated in a particular way. In most fuels, energy is released by **combustion** (burning). Common fuels which produce energy by

urning are paper, wood, **natural gas**, petrol and
oal.

fuel + **oxygen** (often from the air)→
carbon dioxide + water + energy

Nuclear fuels, like **uranium** and plutonium,
roduce energy when their **atoms** undergo
uclear **fission**.

ungus An organism which lacks chlorophyll,
eaves and true roots and which lives as a
arasite or a saprophyte (i.e. it feeds on dead
natter). Examples are mushrooms, moulds and
easts. See **biodegradable**.

use A device in an electric **circuit** which melts
nd cuts off the supply of electricity if the **cur-
ent** becomes too large. This might be due to a
ault or an attempt to overload the system.

Nearly all conductors resist the flow of **charge**;
ne result is an **energy** transfer which causes the
mperature of the conductor to increase. This
called the heating effect of a current.

Household fuses come in various ratings of
nperes and are designed to melt if the current
the circuit rises above a particular value.

o choose the correct fuse for an appliance which
as a **power**, P, in **watts**, use the equation:

$$I = P/250$$

and select a fuse which has a value slightly higher than *I*. We now often use automati switches called *circuit breakers* rather than fuse at currents higher than 13 amperes. The user ca reset the switch after the fault is found an remedied.

The fuse protects the wires of the circuit an the appliance. It should be connected to the live wire. See **three-pin plug**.

fusion (nuclear fusion) The joining of two o more light atomic **nuclei** to make a more mass ive one whose **mass** is slightly lower than th combined masses of the particles it is made from This process involves a large transfer of mass t **energy**. Much of the energy from the sun an other stars comes from fusion.

$$^2_1H + ^2_1H \rightarrow ^3_2He + ^1_0n + energy$$

Fusion is used in an uncontrolled way in th hydrogen atom bomb. Effective ways of control ling this have not yet been developed; however, i promises to be a cheap and clean source of powe in the future.

galaxy Millions of **stars** which appear as group in the sky. Our **solar system** is within galaxy which is called the *milky way*. The mil lions of stars in the milky way appear as a lumi nous band which encircles the heavens.

gamete A reproductive **cell** whose **nucleus** contains only half of the normal number of **chromosomes** *(haploid)*, because these cells are produced by the process of double division called *meiosis*. In humans the male gametes are **spermatazoa** and the female gametes are **ova**.

During **fertilization** male and female gametes fuse to form a *zygote*. The nucleus of the zygote contains the normal number of chromosomes *(diploid)*.

gamete Formation of a zygote in humans.

gamma radiation (γ) High-energy (short wavelength) **electromagnetic waves** produced during the decay of certain **nuclei** (see **radioactivity**). **Energy** leaves as a packet of radiation (sometimes called a *quantum* or *photon*), and the nucleus becomes more stable.

Gamma radiation can pass through matter very easily. It forms **ions** when it collides with **atoms** of the material and slowly loses energy. It is able to penetrate deep into the human body and may cause disorders such as cancers. Workers dealing with materials which emit gamma radiation must be protected by lead and/or concrete shielding. *Gamma radiography* is used to examine the internal structure of metal objects such as aircraft engine components. Faults which are not visible in an exterior examination can be detected and the component replaced before the engine fails.

gas or **vapour** The normal **state of matter** whose particles have the highest **energy**. When **heat** is supplied to a **liquid** the **atoms** or **molecules** are given **kinetic energy**. This may be enough to overcome the forces of attraction which hold the particles together in the **liquid** state. If this happens the liquid boils and turns to gas. Collisions of gas particles on the walls of a container exert a **pressure**. The particles move quickly, at hundreds of metres per second, in random directions and fill all the space available. The **density** of a gas is much less (e.g. 1/1000 times) than a **solid** or a liquid. Natural gas is a major energy **resource**.

gas exchange In this process organisms exchange gases with the **environment** for the purposes of **metabolism**. Most organisms need a continuous supply of **oxygen** for the energy-producing reaction of **respiration**.

glucose + oxygen → **energy** + **carbon dioxide** + **water**

In addition to this green plants need carbon dioxide for **photosynthesis**.

$$\text{carbon dioxide} + \text{water} \xrightarrow{\text{light energy}} \textbf{carbohydrate} + \text{oxygen}$$

Both reactions use and produce gases which are exchanged between the organism and the atmosphere (land organisms) or water (aquatic organisms).

$$\text{oxygen} \underset{\text{photosynthesis}}{\overset{\text{respiration}}{\rightleftarrows}} \text{carbon dioxide} + \text{water}$$

The gas-exchange surfaces within organisms have certain characteristics which allow the exchange to take place.

a) A large surface area for maximum gas exchange.

b) The surface is thin to allow **diffusion**.

c) The surface is moist as gas exchange takes place in solution.

d) In animals, the surface has a good **blood** supply as it is the blood which transports gases to and from the cells of the body.

In mammals gas exchange occurs across the alveoli in the **lungs**. It is the result of differences between the concentrations of oxygen and carbon dioxide in the air inside the alveoli and the deoxygenated blood in the **capillaries** around the alveoli. These differences in concentration are called *concentration gradients*. These gradients cause oxygen to diffuse from the alveoli into **red blood cells** in the capillary, and carbon dioxide to diffuse out of the blood into the alveoli. See **breathing**.

Alveoli and associated blood vessels

deoxygenated blood from heart

oxygenated blood to heart

Gas exchange in the alveolus

oxygen

red blood cells

blood capillary

carbon dioxide

(a)

(b)

gas exchange (a) Alveoli and associated blood vessels. (b) Gas exchange in the alveolus.

general formula A formula used in organic chemistry which shows the relative numbers of the different **atoms** in terms of a variable n for all of the members of a group of **compounds**. The actual formula for any particular compound in the group is found by substituting a number for *n*. For example; the general formula for the group of compounds called alkanes is C_nH_{2n+2}. The formula for each member of the alkanes is obtained by substituting for *n*.

n	Name of compound	Molecular formula of compound
1	methane	CH_4
2	ethane	C_2H_6
3	propane	C_3H_8
4	butane	C_4H_{10}
etc.		

A series of compounds with the same general formula is sometimes referred to as a *homologous series*. See **hydrocarbons**.

generator A machine which converts **kinetic energy** to **electricity**. *Alternators* give **alternating current**; other types of generator give **direct current**. Simple forms of both AC and DC generators have a similar structure.

See **electromagnetic induction**.

genes The subunits of **chromosomes**. They consist of lengths of **DNA** and control the hereditary characteristics of organisms. A single gene consists of up to 1000 *base pairs* in a DNA mol-

ecule. The sequence of the base pairs represents coded information known as the *genetic code*. This code determines the structures of the different types of **proteins**, particularly **enzymes**, synthesized by the **cell**. In turn, these determine the structure and function of the cells and **tissues**, and ultimately the organism.

The genetic code is an arrangement of *nitrogen base pairs* in DNA. Each group of three adjacent base pairs (called triplets) is responsible within the cell for linking together **amino acids** to form protein. For example, the base triplet GTA codes for the amino acid *histidine* while GTT codes for another amino acid, *glutamine*.

The sequence and type of amino acids determine the nature of the protein. Consider two fruit flies (*Drosophila*): one has a light body colour controlled by a gene X, and the other a dark body colour controlled by a gene Y.

gene X ——————→ enzyme X ——————→ pigment X light
    synthesizes   catalyses the   body
                         formation of

gene Y ——————→ enzyme Y ——————→ pigment Y dark
    synthesizes   catalyses the   bod
                         formation of

See **allele**.

genetic engineering The deliberate alteration of the genetic information on the **chromosomes**

of an organism in order to bring about some advantage to people. This technique has been used successfully to produce microorganisms which can synthesize useful drugs, such as **insulin**. In the future it may be possible to improve the food potential of animals and plants by engineering qualities such as high yields and resistance to disease.

geothermal aquifer   A source of hot water from the ground which may be used for heating. In some parts of the world there are very hot rocks quite close to the surface. As rain water percolates through these rocks it is heated. If the geology of the location is suitable, the hot water collects in deposits which can be tapped off by drilling down into the rocks. See **geothermal hot dry rock structures**, **renewable energy sources**.

geothermal hot dry rock structures   Rock structures from which heat energy can be removed. The rocks are hot but have no water associated with them (see **geothermal aquifer**). Two wells are drilled down to the rocks, ending several hundred metres apart. The permeability of the rock between the ends of the wells is increased by applying hydraulic **pressure** which enlarges natural fissures in the rock.

Cold water is forced down one well and passes

through the fissures in the hot rocks between the ends of the wells. As it passes through the fissures it is heated and hot water is collected from the second well. See **renewable energy sources**.

geothermal hot dry rock structures

germination The first stage in the **growth** of **spores** and **seeds**. This often follows a period of dormancy and normally requires particular environmental conditions such as the availability of **water** and **oxygen** and a favourable **temperature**. If these conditions are not present, spores and seeds can remain alive for some time (often years) before germinating. In this state they are said to be *dormant*.

Seed germination in flowering plants. There are two types of germination; hypogeal and epigeal. The difference lies in what happens to the cotyledons. In epigeal germination the cotyledons become the first leaves of the new plant, while in hypogeal germination they do not. In both cases water is absorbed through the micropyle, the testa splits open and the radicle emerges.

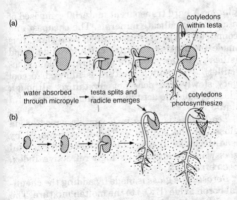

germination (a) Hypogeal germination (broad bean). (b) Epigeal germination (French bean).

gestation period See **pregnancy**.

giant structure Structures of **atoms** or **ions** in which there are large numbers of particles present in a crystal lattice. Each particle has a strong force of attraction for the particles around it. Giant structures tend to have high **melting** and **boiling points**. **Ionic compounds**, **metals** and some **nonmetals** have giant structures. Compare **molecule**.

glass A hard transparent material composed of a mixture of silicate minerals. The cheapest and commonest type of glass is called *soda glass*. It is made by heating together calcium oxide, sand (silica), sodium carbonate and scrap broken glass (cullet). The molten mixture is allowed to cool very slowly and does not crystallize: although glass is solid, it actually has the structure of a liquid.

Lead glass is made in a similar way to soda glass but the sodium carbonate is replaced by lead (II) oxide. It is used to make quality crystal glassware because of its high refractive index. See **refraction**.

Borosilicate glass is made by adding the chemical boron oxide (B_2O_5) to the molten mixture. The resulting glass does not expand very much when heated and it can be heated and cooled rapidly without cracking. It is sold under trade names such as 'Pyrex'® and has a variety of uses including kitchenware and laboratory apparatus.

glucose A monosaccharide **carbohydrate** made during **photosynthesis**. This substance is an important **energy** source in both animal and plant **cells**. See **respiration**.

glycogen This is a polysaccharide **carbohydrate**. It consists of branched chains of **glucose** units. It is important in animals as a short-term energy store. In vertebrates glycogen is stored in **muscle** and **liver cells**. It can be rapidly converted to glucose by the action of amylase **enzymes** if the level of glucose in the blood is too low. See **insulin**.

gravity A **force**, the attraction between **masses**. The cause of gravity is not known. The **weight** of an object depends on the value of the gravitational attraction and its mass. Gravity is taken to act through a point at the centre of an object where we imagine the object's mass to be concentrated. This point is sometimes called the *centre of gravity* or *centre of mass*.

greenhouse effect The effect created by **heat radiation** from **earth** being reflected back to earth by the **atmosphere**. **Temperatures** around the world have shown a small but significant increase over the last century. Some scientists believe that this is linked to the increasing concentration of **carbon dioxide** in the atmosphere. The earth receives heat radiation from the **sun**. Some of this is absorbed by the earth and re-emitted back into space at a longer wavelength. The atmosphere reflects some of the re-emitted radiation back on the earth and prevents it from going into space. The more carbon dioxide there is in the atmosphere the more heat radiation is reflected back to earth, hence the hotter the earth will become. A similar effect happens in a greenhouse; the glass reflects re-emitted heat radiation back into the greenhouse (hence the name of this effect).

greenhouse effect

The increasing concentration of carbon dioxide in the atmosphere is a result of the combustion of increasing quantities of **fossil fuels** and the large scale deforestation in many parts of the world (less vegetation, therefore less **photosyn-**

thesis). The greenhouse effect is a serious problem because it is believed to be responsible for changes in the climate of some areas of the world and it may result in an increase in the sea level as part of the ice caps melt.

group In the **periodic table** the **elements** are arranged in horizontal *periods* and vertical groups.

group I	lithium, sodium, potassium
group II	beryllium, magnesium, **calcium**
group III	boron, **aluminium**
group IV	**carbon**, silicon
group V	nitrogen, phosphorus
group VI	**oxygen**, **sulphur**
group VII	fluorine, **chlorine**, bromine
group 0	helium, neon, argon

In each group the outermost electron shell contains the same number of **electrons** for each member. The number of electrons is the same as the group number.

growth The increase in size and complexity of an organism during its development from **embryo** to maturity. It is the result of **cell** division, cell elongation and cell differentiation. In plants growth originates at certain localized areas called *meristems*. In animals growth goes on all over the body.

habitat The place where an animal or plant lives. Organisms are adapted to the particular environmental conditions (see **environment**) within a habitat.

half-life period ($t_{\frac{1}{2}}$) The time it takes for a measure, whose **decay** is exponential, to fall to half of its value. Half-life is often used in connection with the number of parent radioactive **nuclei** in a sample.

half-life period The number of parent radioactive nuclei in a sample will decrease by half every $t_{\frac{1}{2}}$ period.

halogens A collective name for the **elements** in **group VII** of the **periodic table**. They are all poisonous nonmetallic elements. At room temperature fluorine and **chlorine** are gases, bromine is a liquid and iodine is a solid. All the halogens are oxidizing agents (see **oxidation**);

their oxidizing power and chemical reactivity decreases as we go down the group, i.e.

$$F_2 > Cl_2 > Br_2 > I_2$$

They react vigorously with **metals** and **hydrogen** forming *halides*:

> fluorine → fluorides
> chlorine → chlorides
> bromine → bromides
> iodine → iodides

They all contain seven **electrons** in the outer shell of the **atom** and form **ions** with a single negative charge (*univalent anions*) e.g. Cl^-, Br^-.

hardness of water The concentration of dissolved calcium and magnesium salts in water. Water from the mains supply is often described as being hard or soft depending on how well it lathers with soap. Soft water lathers easily with small amounts of soap whereas hard water does not. Hard water forms a scum and requires more soap than soft water to produce a lather.

Hardness in water is caused by calcium and magnesium salts which are dissolved in the water when it flows over rocks such as limestone, chalk and gypsum. The **metal ions** are responsible for the hardness since they react chemically with the soap to form the scum. Soft water collects in areas of the country where the rocks are insoluble in water, e.g. the granite areas such as the Lake District, Cornwall and the Highlands of Scotland. There are two distinct types of hard water.

(a) *Temporary hard water*. This contains dissolved calcium hydrogencarbonate due to slightly acidic rain dissolving chalk and limestone.

$$H_2O(l) + CO_2(g) \rightarrow H_2CO_3(aq)$$
water　　carbon dioxide　　carbonic acid

$$CaCO_3(s) + H_2CO_3 \rightarrow Ca(HCO_3)_2(aq)$$
calcium carbonate　　carbonic acid　　calcium hydrogencarbonate

It is called temporary hardness because it can be removed simply by boiling the water. This reverses the above reactions and results in insoluble calcium carbonate being deposited. In temporary hard water areas the calcium carbonate causes problems as lime scale in kettles and boilers.

(b) *Permanent hard water*. This contains dissolved calcium sulphate and magnesium sulphate. These chemicals cannot be removed by boiling but are removed by adding washing soda (sodium carbonate). This precipitates them as insoluble carbonates.

heart A muscular pumping organ which maintains the circulation of **blood** around the body. It usually contains valves which prevent the blood from flowing backwards. In mammals the heart has four chambers; two relatively thin-walled atria (auricles) which receive blood, and two thicker-walled ventricles which pump blood out. The right side of the heart deals only with deoxygenated blood and the left side only with oxygenated blood. The wall of the left ventricle is thicker and more powerful than that of the right since it pumps blood to all parts of the body, whereas the right ventricle only pumps blood to the **lungs**. See **circulatory system**, **heartbeat**.

heart

heartbeat This is the result of alternative contraction and relaxation of the **heart**. In mammals it consists of two distinct phases:

(a) *Diastole*. The atria and ventricles relax. This allows blood to flow from the atria into the ventricles.

(b) *Systole*. The ventricles contract, forcing **blood** into the pulmonary **artery** and the aorta. At the same time the relaxed atria fill with blood ready for the next beat.

heartbeat Relaxation and contraction of heart (right side).

Heartbeat is initiated by a structure in the right atrium called the *pacemaker*, although the rate is controlled by a part of the **brain** called the medulla oblongata. This part of the brain monitors the activity of the body by detecting increases in the **carbon dioxide** level in the blood; the result of increased **respiration** (caused by increased activity). It is also affected by certain **hormones** such as adrenaline from the adrenal glands. The rate of human heartbeat is measured by counting the **pulse rate**. People with heart defects are sometimes fitted with electronic pacemakers.

heat   A form of **energy**. It is the internal energy possessed as the movement of **molecules** of a substance (see **kinetic energy**). The word is also used to mean energy transfer. Thus when we heat a beaker of water with a bunsen burner there is energy transfer from the burning **gas** to increase the particle motion in the **water**. Heat transfer may be by **conduction** (thermal), **convection** or **radiation**.

homeostasis   A general term for the maintenance of constant conditions within an organism. For example:
(a) control of **blood glucose** level by **insulin**;
(b) control of blood water content by ADH;
(c) control of body **temperature** by the **skin**, etc.
   See **hormones**.

Hooke's law   The law which states that when an elastic object, like a rubber band, is stretched, the increase in its length is proportional to the **force** applied; provided this force does not exceed the *elastic limit*. For example, if a force of 10 N increased the length of a rubber band by 1 cm then a force of 20 N would result in an increase of 2 cm. If the elastic limit is exceeded the object ceases to be elastic and no longer obeys Hooke's law. See **elasticity**.

hormones Chemicals which are secreted by the **endocrine glands** and are transported via the bloodstream to certain target **organs**. At these organs the hormones cause specific effects which are vital in regulating and coordinating the activities of the body. Hormones are sometimes called *chemical messengers*. Hormone action is usually slower than nervous stimulation. The following tables summarize the properties of some important human hormones, but there are many others.

Endocrine gland	Hormone	Effects
Pituitary gland	ADH (Anti-diuretic Hormone)	Controls water reabsorption by the **kidneys**.
	TSH (Thyroid Stimulating Hormone)	Stimulates *Thyroxine* production in the thyroid gland.
	FSH (Follicle-stimulating Hormone)	Causes ova to mature and the ovaries to produce oestrogen.
	LH (Luteinizing Hormone)	Initiates ovulation and causes the ovaries to release progesterone.

	Growth hormone	Stimulates growth in young animals. In humans, deficiency causes dwarfism and excess causes gigantism.
Thyroid gland	*Thyroxin*	Controls rate of growth and development in young animals. In human infants, deficiency causes *cretinism*. Controls the rate of chemical activity in adults. Excess causes thinness and over-activity, and deficiency causes obesity and sluggishness.
Pancreas (*Islets of Langerhans*)	Insulin	Stimulates conversion of **glucose** to **glycogen** in the **liver**. Deficiency causes *diabetes*.
Adrenal glands	*Adrenaline*	Under conditions of '*fight, flight,* or *fright*' causes changes which increase the efficiency of the animal. For example, increased heartbeat and breathing, diversion of blood from gut to muscles, conversion of glycogen in the liver to glucose.

Endocrine gland	Hormone	Effects
Ovaries	Oestrogen	Stimulates **secondary sexual characteristics** in the female, for example, breast development. Causes the uterus wall to thicken during menstrual cycle.
	Progesterone	Prepares uterus for implantation.
Testes	*Testosterone*	Stimulates secondary sexual characteristics in the male, for example, facial hair.

humus A general term for organic material in **soil**, consisting of decomposing plant and animal remains. It is a desirable feature of soils as it provides plants, and ultimately animals, with nutrients.

hybrid A plant or animal produced as a result of a cross between two parents who are genetically unlike each other, or between two differing but related organisms.

hydrocarbon A **compound** which contains only **hydrogen** and **carbon**. There are three main series of hydrocarbons.

Name of series	General formula	Examples	
Alkanes	C_nH_{2n+2}	methane	CH_4
		ethane	C_2H_6
		propane	C_3H_8
Alkenes	C_nH_{2n}	ethene	C_2H_4
		propene	C_3H_6
Alkynes	C_nH_{2n-2}	ethyne	C_2H_2
		propyne	C_3H_4

hydrochloric acid   A strong acid made by dissolving *hydrogen chloride* (HCl) gas in water. Hydrogen chloride gas can be made by reacting the **elements** together directly or by reacting sodium chloride with concentrated **sulphuric acid**.

$$H_2(g) + Cl_2(g) \rightarrow 2HCl(g)$$
$$NaCl(s) + H_2SO_4(l) \rightarrow NaHSO_4(s) + HCl(g)$$

The gas reacts with **ammonia** to form dense white fumes of ammonium chloride.

$$NH_3(g) + HCl(g) \rightarrow NH_4Cl(s)$$

The **atoms** in hydrogen chloride gas are held together by **covalent bonds**; however, **ions** are formed when it dissolves in a *polar* solvent such as water, hence hydrochloric acid is an ionic compound and contains hydrogen (H^+) and chloride (Cl^-) ions.

Hydrogen chloride gas is very soluble in water. The maximum **concentration** of the solution is 36% (about 11 **moles/dm^3**). The acid is *monobasic* and produces **salts** called chlorides.

$$Fe(s) + 2HCl(aq) \rightarrow FeCl_2(aq) + H_2(g)$$
$$Mg(s) + 2HCl(aq) \rightarrow MgCl_2(aq) + H_2(g)$$

The acid releases **carbon dioxide** from carbonates and can be oxidized to **chlorine**.

$$Na_2CO_3(s) + 2HCl(aq) \rightarrow 2NaCl(aq) + CO_2(g) + H_2O(l)$$
$$MnO_2(s) + 4HCl(aq) \rightarrow MnCl_2(aq) + 2H_2O(l) + Cl_2(g)$$

hydroelectricity Electrical power produced by using the **energy** of falling **water**, often from behind a dam.

hydrogen (H_2) A reactive **element** which is a diatomic **gas**. An **atom** of the commonest isotope of hydrogen consists of a **nucleus** of one **proton** and, outside the nucleus, one orbiting **electron**. Hydrogen has two other **isotopes**, *deuterium* and *tritium*, whose nuclei also contain one and two **neutrons** respectively. Hydrogen can form **covalent bonds** by sharing electrons; e.g.

$$2H_2(g) + O_2(g) \rightarrow 2H_2O(g)$$
$$C_2H_4(g) + H_2(g) \rightarrow C_2H_6(g) \ (hydrogenation)$$

Hydrogen ions (H^+) are produced when hydrogen **atoms** lose their electrons. (Under the right conditions a hydrogen atom can produce hydride ions, H^-). **Acids** contain hydrogen ions. Hydrogen is a reducing agent. It is used to convert vegetable oils into *margarine*.

Industrially, hydrogen is made from **petroleum** by the *steam reformation of alkanes*. Large quantities of hydrogen are used in the formation of **ammonia** by the *Haber process*. In the laboratory hydrogen is made by reacting a **metal** with an acid other than nitric acid. Zinc and dilute **hydrochloric acid** are commonly used.

$$Zn(s) + 2HCl(aq) \rightarrow ZnCl_2(aq) + H_2(g)$$

Hydrogen is also released by the **electrolysis** of aqueous solutions which contain ions of elements above hydrogen in the **electrochemical series**, e.g. $NaCl(aq)$, $Mg(NO_3)_2(aq)$, and by the reaction of **water** with **group** I and group II metals, e.g. sodium, calcium.

Hydrogen is highly inflammable and forms explosive mixtures with **oxygen**. It has a very low **density**, and was once used in balloons and airships, however several large-scale disasters occurred due to its highly inflammable nature.

hydrogen ion (H^+) A positively charged **ion** (which is, in fact, a **proton**) formed when a hydrogen atom loses its **electron**.

$$H \rightarrow H^+ + e^-$$

This small particle is very reactive. In aqueous

solution it combines with a **molecule** of **water** to form an *oxonium ion*.

$$H^+ + H_2O \rightarrow H_3O^+$$

All aqueous solutions of **acids** contain more hydrogen ions than **hydroxide ions**. The **pH** of a solution is a measure of the **concentration** of hydrogen ions in it.

hydroxide (OH⁻) Found in all **alkalis** and in alkaline solutions, e.g. sodium hydroxide Na^+OH^-. It is present, to a small extent, in all aqueous solutions because of the **dissociation** of **water**.

$$\begin{array}{ccccc} H_2O & \rightarrow & H^+ & + & OH^- \\ \text{water} & & \textbf{hydrogen} & & \text{hydroxide ion} \end{array}$$

Solutions which contain more hydroxide ions than hydrogen ions are described as alkaline. These have a **pH** greater than 7.

igneous rocks Rocks formed by the crystallization of molten material, called *magma*, which comes up from deep in the earth. Igneous rocks are classified according to their grain size and composition. Composition is often thought of as ranging from acidic to basic because of the nature of the different minerals present.

	Acidic		Basic	
Coarse grain	Granite	Diorite	Gabbro	Peridotite
Fine grain	Felsite		Basalt	

See **rock cycle**.

immunization The introduction of **antigens** into the body in the form of a **vaccine**. This produces an *immune response* to that antigen, thus protecting the person against future attack by the same type of antigen. In Britain, all parents have the opportunity to have their children immunized against a variety of diseases. Babies are normally immunized against diphtheria, tetanus, whooping cough, polio, measles and mumps. All girls are immunized against rubella. All teenagers are immunized against tuberculosis.

incubator A device for maintaining a constant **temperature** suitable for the **growth** and development of bacterial cultures. The temperature is often set at around human body temperature, 36.9 °C. Incubators are also used for hatching eggs.

indicator A substance which turns different colours according to acidic and alkaline conditions. It can be used to show whether a solution is an **acid** or an **alkali**.

Indicator	Colour in acid	Neutral	Colour in alkali
litmus	red		blue
phenophthalein	colourless		red
universal	red orange yellow	green	blue purple

infrared A region of the **spectrum of electromagnetic waves**. The approximate wavelength range is 10^{-6}–10^{-3}m, and the approximate **frequency** range 10^{12}–10^{15} Hz.

Infrared **radiation** is thermal or heat radiation. It is detectable by blackened **thermometers**, **skin nerve cells**, thermopiles and photographic films. All matter radiates infrared at all times.

inherited diseases Diseases resulting from **genes** which produce harmful effects. These genes may be dominant or recessive (see **allele**). When the disease is caused by a recessive gene, carriers may transfer the disease to the next generation without, themselves, suffering from its effects. *Cystic fibrosis* is a serious defect of the **pancreas** caused by a recessive gene. Some inherited diseases, such as the blood disease *haemophilia*, are associated with genes on the sex **chromosomes**.

inorganic chemistry A branch of chemistry concerned with the study of those aspects which do not fall within the study of **organic chemistry**. It is the study of **elements** and their **compounds**. This includes the chemistry of some compounds of the element **carbon**, such as its oxides, metal carbonates and hydrogen-carbonates, but excludes all organic compounds such as alcohols, esters and **hydrocarbons**.

insulation A technique to reduce the **energy** transfer from one place to another. Thus *thermal insulation*:
(a) Reduces **heat** energy losses from a high temperature area such as an oven.
(b) Reduces heat energy gains to a low temperature area such as a refrigerator.

In cold climates people use many methods of insulation to reduce heat loss from their homes. These may include *double glazing, cavity wall insulation* and *loft insulation*, making use of such materials as *fibre-glass, polystyrene* and *mineral wool*. Electrical insulation often involves coating conductors with **nonmetals**, such as plastics, to prevent **charge** (and thus energy) being transferred anywhere other than along the conductor.

Metals are good conductors of both thermal and electrical energy. Their value in insulation is limited to use as reflectors of **radiation**.

insulin A **hormone** which is secreted by the Islets of Langerhans in the **pancreas** of vertebrates.

Insulin regulates the conversion of **glucose** into **glycogen** which occurs in the **liver**. If the concentration of glucose in the **blood** is high, the rate of secretion of insulin is high. Thus glucose is rapidly converted into glycogen for storage in the liver. Conversely, if the concentration of glucose in the blood is low, less insulin is secreted, and less glucose is converted into glycogen. This is an example of the **feedback** regulation associated with many hormones. People suffering from *diabetes* are unable to produce enough insulin to control the delicate glucose level balance in their bodies.

insulin A hormone which controls the conversion of glucose into glycogen.

intestine This is the region of the **alimentary canal** between the stomach and the anus or cloaca. In vertebrates, most **digestion** and **absorption** of food occur in the intestine which is usually differentiated into the small intestine and the large intestine.

ion An **atom** which has become electrically charged by gaining or losing **electrons**. *Cations* are positively charged, e.g. Na^+, and *anions* are negatively charged, e.g. O^{2-}. Atoms tend to lose or gain electrons to produce an ion with the same *electronic configurations* as a **noble gas**. Groups of atoms (radicals) may also form ions.

sulphate SO_4^{2-}	nitrate NO_3^-
hydroxide OH^-	ammonium NH_4^+

ionic bonds Chemical bonds which occur because of *electrostatic* attractive forces between positively and negatively charged **ions**. Ionic bonds are often present in **compounds** of nonmetals from **groups VI and VII** and **metals**, e.g. Na^+Cl^-, $Mg^{2+}(Br^-)$ and in compounds containing, *radicals* such as sulphate and nitrate, e.g. $Cu^{2+}SO_4^{2-}$, $K^+NO_3^-$.

ionic compounds Compounds which contain **ionic bonds**. They tend to have high **melting** and **boiling points** and are conductors of electricity when molten.

ionizing radiations Radiations which can remove **electrons** from **atoms**, thus creating **ions**. This may be caused by **alpha** and **beta**

particles, gamma rays (see **gamma radiation**) and **X-rays** (**neutrons** cause ionization indirectly).

iron The most widely used metallic **element**, although it is usually encountered as **steel alloys**. In this form it is used for building girders, car bodies, cans, tools and many other items of everyday life.

Iron is extracted from **ores** such as haematite (Fe_2O_3) and magnetite (Fe_3O_4) by reduction with carbon monoxide in a **blast furnace**. The iron produced in a blast furnace is brittle. To make it useful it is converted into a range of different steels with varying properties.

A major problem in using iron and many steels is **corrosion** (**rust**). The iron oxidizes in moist **air** to produce a soft crumbly oxide.

$$\text{iron} \xrightarrow{\text{moist air}} \text{iron (II) oxide } (Fe_2O_3)$$

Iron is a transition metal and can have **valency** 2 or 3. It reacts with dilute **acids** to form iron (II) **compounds**, e.g.

$$Fe(s) + 2HCl(aq) \rightarrow FeCl_2(aq) + H_2(g)$$

Small amounts of iron (in the form of iron compounds) are an essential part of the human diet. It is needed by the body to make the pigment haemoglobin which gives the red colour to **red blood cells**.

isotopes Species of the same chemical element. They have the same number of **protons** but different numbers of **neutrons** in their nuclei. The following table shows some details of some isotopes of **carbon**.

	Number of protons	Number of neutrons
carbon-12	6	6
carbon-13	6	7
carbon-14	6	8

joint The point in a **skeleton** where two or more **bones** meet. Some joints allow movement. There are three main types of movable joint in mammals.

joint Ball and socket joint.

(a) *Ball and socket joint.* This allows movement in several planes. In humans the shoulder and hip are ball and socket joints.

(b) *Hinge joint.* This allows movement in only one plane. In humans the elbow and knee are hinge joints.

joint Hinge joints.

(c) *Gliding joint.* This type of joint occurs when two flat surfaces are able to glide over each other, allowing only a small amount of movement. In humans the wrist and ankle are gliding joints.

joint Gliding joint.

The ends of bones at movable joints are covered in *cartilage* to reduce **friction** as the bones rub against each other.

joule (J) The unity of **energy** and work. 1 joule of work is done when a **force** of 1 newton moves 1 metre.

Kelvin scale A scale of **temperature** sometimes used in preference to the Celsius (or centigrade) scale. The Celsius scale is positive above the **melting point** of ice (0°C) and negative below it. Celsius is a widely used scale; however, in some fields of study, such as low temperature physics, negative values are a disadvantage. The Kelvin (or absolute) scale does not have negative values since its zero is at *absolute zero*. To convert Celsius temperature to Kelvin temperature add 273, i.e.:

$$0\,°C = 273 \text{ K}$$
$$100\,°C = 373 \text{ K}$$

kidney An **organ** found in vertebrates which consists of a collection of units called *nephrons*. It is concerned with **excretion** and **osmoregulation**. In humans, the kidneys are a pair of red-

kidney Position.

kidney Section.

brown oval structures at the back of the abdomen.

Oxygenated **blood** enters each kidney via the renal **artery** and deoxygenated blood leaves by the renal **vein**. A tube called the *ureter* connects each kidney with the bladder.

Within the kidney the renal artery divides into many small blood vessels called *arterioles* which terminate in tiny knots of blood **capillaries** called *glomeruli*. There are about one million glomeruli in a human kidney. Each is enclosed in a cup-shaped organ called a *Bowman's capsule*.

kidney Bowman's capsule and glomerulus.

Two processes occur in the kidneys:

(a) *Ultrafiltration*. The blood vessel leaving the glomerulus is narrower than the one entering it. This puts the blood within the glomerulus under high **pressure**. Under these conditions the capillary wall acts as a selectively permeable membrane. Blood components which have only small molecules are forced through it into the Bowman's capsule while components with larger molecules remain in the blood.

Large molecules remaining in the blood	Small molecules filtered out of the blood
blood **cells**	glucose
plasma proteins	urea
	mineral salts
	water
	amino acids

(b) *Reabsorption*. The fluid filtered from the blood passes from the Bowman's capsule down the renal tubule. Each tubule is supplied with a network of blood vessels and as the fluid passes through it useful materials are reabsorbed into the blood. These will include all the glucose and amino acids and some mineral salts and water.

By the time the liquid reaches the end of the

renal tubule it consists of a solution of urea and mineral salts. It drains into the bladder via the ureter and is eventually expelled from the body as **urine**. The amount of water which is reabsorbed is controlled by a **hormone**, called the antidiuretic hormone (ADH). It is released by the pituitary gland, which monitors the amount of

kidney   Reabsorption.

water in the blood. If the level of water is too low more ADH is released into the bloodstream. This results in more water being reabsorbed by the kidneys, leaving the urine more concentrated. If the level of water is too high the converse occurs.

kidney The pituitary gland controls production of ADH.

kinetic energy The type of **energy** existing in a moving object. The amount depends on the object's **mass** m and its **speed** v as follows;

$$\text{kinetic energy} = \tfrac{1}{2}\,\text{mass} \times \text{speed}^2$$
$$W = \tfrac{1}{2}mv^2$$

kinetic model A theory about the structure of matter which is commonly accepted by scientists. It is described by the following four statements:
(a) All matter is made of particles.
(b) The particles are always moving.
(c) The particles attract each other.
(d) The **temperature** of a substance relates to

the mean **energy** of its particles.

The kinetic theory is able to explain the behaviour of matter. See **conduction, convection, diffusion, evaporation, expansion, states of matter**.

landfill gas An inflammable mixture of **gases** obtained when certain waste materials are buried in the ground and allowed to decompose by bacterial action. This **renewable energy source** is a significant source of **energy** in the USA but has been less well exploited in Britain to date.

latent heat Hidden **heat**. It is the **energy** involved in changes of **state**. If heat is added, at a constant rate, to a **solid**, the **temperature**/time graph has shape (a). A similar graph for a **liquid** gradually losing heat at a constant rate has shape (b).

latent heat Temperature/time graphs.

In each case, the temperature stays constant while the change of state takes place. A similar situation exists in the changes from liquid to **gas** and gas to liquid. The quantity of energy transferred to or from the particles during changes of state depends on the nature of the substance and its state.

lead A metallic **element** in **group** IV of the **periodic table**. It is a soft grey **metal** and has a high **density**. The main source of lead is the ore galena (PbS). Lead and its **alloys** are widely used, e.g. in the lead-acid accumulator solders, and as flashing on roofs to keep out water. Lead absorbs **radiation** from radioactive **isotopes** and **X-rays**. It is used for screening and containing radioactive sources to protect people from the effects of radiation. Lead can be used to store highly corrosive chemicals such as **sulphuric acid**.

At one time lead was widely used for water pipes, and some of its **compounds** were the basis of paints; however, studies have shown that even very small amounts of lead absorbed into the body can damage a person's health. A lead compound, tetraethyl lead, is still used as an antiknock agent in petrol (making the engine run more smoothly), however, because of the danger to health, many car manufacturers are designing cars which can use other antiknock agents.

leaf The part of a flowering plant which grows from the **stem**. It is typically flat and green, and contains **chlorophyll**. The functions of a leaf are:

(a) **Photosynthesis**.
(b) **Gas exchange**.
(c) **Transpiration**.

upper epidermis with cuticle

palisade mesophyll with chloroplasts

spongy mesophyll with fewer chloroplasts and larger air spaces

lower epidermis

guard cell with chloroplasts — stoma

leaf The structure of a typical leaf.

LED Light-emitting diode. This is a p–n junction **diode**, and is usually made from gallium arsenide phosphide. **Energy** is released within the LED and this is given off as **light**. The junction is made near to the surface so that the emitted light can be seen. No light is emitted with a reverse bias. LEDs are commonly coloured red, yellow or green. They are widely used in a variety of electronic devices.

lens An optical device which bends transmitted **light** by **refraction**.

lens The effect of a diverging lens.

(a) *Converging (convex) lenses* bring the rays together at a point called the *focus*. They are thicker at the centre than at the edge.

(b) *Diverging (concave) lenses* spread the rays out so they appear to be coming from one point, the focus. They are thin at the centre but get thicker towards the outside. See **eye**.

converging lenses   diverging lenses

lens Converging and diverging lenses.

leucocyte See **white blood cell**.

lever A type of machine in which a certain **force** applied at one point gives an output force elsewhere. Levers are often grouped into three classes (1, 2 and 3). The classes differ in the positions of the input force (the effort applied) and

Class 1

The pivot is between the load and effort. Usually the effort is smaller than the load because it is further out.

Class 2

The pivot is at the end of the lever and the load is in the middle. A small effort lifts a large load.

Class 3

The pivot is again at the end but the effort is in the middle. There is a *mechanical disadvantage* and a large effort is needed to lift a small load.

lever The three classes of lever.

the output force (the load overcome) relative to the pivot (turning point or fulcrum).

light A region of the **spectrum** of **electro-magnetic waves** which can be seen by the normal human **eye**. It has wavelengths between 400–760 nm. The colour of the light is related to its wavelength. Like all waves, light can be absorbed, reflected, refracted, diffracted and shows interference effects. Like all electromagnetic waves, it travels through empty space at 300 000 000 m/s and this value is commonly called the **speed of light**.

lipids See **fats**.

liquid A **state of matter** in which particles are bonded by intermolecular forces.

The particles are not fixed in a rigid lattice as in a **solid**. During **evaporation** and boiling the particles get enough energy to overcome the intermolecular forces and become a **gas**.

litmus A dye extracted from lichen. It is used as an acid–base **indicator**.

acidic solution	neutral pH = 7	alkaline solution
red ←———————	purple	———————→ blue

liver The largest **organ** of the vertebrate body which occupies much of the upper part of the abdomen where it is in close association with the **alimentary canal**. The liver is an important organ and has many functions. Some of the main ones are listed below.

(a) Production of **bile** for use in digestion.
(b) Deamination of **amino acids** which are excess to the needs of the body.
(c) Regulation of **blood sugar** by the inter-conversion of **glucose** and **glycogen**.
(d) Storage of **iron** and **vitamins** A and D.
(e) Detoxification of poisonous substances.
(f) Release and distribution of **heat** production by the chemical activity of liver cells.
(g) Conversion of stored **fat** for use by the tissues.
(h) Manufacture of the **plasma** protein fibrino-gen which is involved in **blood clotting**.

logic gate A circuit, widely used in computers, which performs a single logic action. The output from a logic gate depends on the combination of inputs. There are four fundamental logic gates: AND, OR, XOR and NOT. The output of a logic gate, for all possible combinations of inputs, is often shown in a *truth table*.

A NOT gate may be combined with the other fundamental gates to give NAND, NOR and NXOR gates.

All logic gates in *integrated circuits* are made by combinations of NAND and NOR gates. For example:

logic gate	truth table

an AND gate

Input		Output
0	0	0
0	1	0
1	0	0
1	1	1

an OR gate

Input		Output
0	0	0
0	1	1
1	0	1
1	1	1

an X–OR gate

Input		Output
0	0	0
0	1	1
1	0	1
1	1	0

a NOT gate

Input	Output
0	1
1	0

logic gate   Truth table.

logic gate NAND, NOR and NXOR gates.

logic gate AND and OR gates constructed from NAND gates.

lungs The breathing **organs** of mammals amphibians, reptiles and birds. In mammals th lungs are two elastic sacs located in the thorax They can be expanded or compressed by move ments of the thorax in such a way that air is continually taken in (inhaled) and expelled (exhaled).

Air is taken into the body through the windpipe (trachea). The trachea divides into two bronchi which enter the lungs. Each bronchus then further divides into smaller bronchioles, which eventually terminate as millions of air-sacs called *alveoli*. The alveoli are richly supplied with **blood capillaries**, and **gases** are able to diffuse into and out of the bloodstream. See **breathing in mammals**, **gas exchange**.

trachea
rings of cartilage
bronchus
bronchioles

lungs Air passages in the lungs.

magma Molten material coming from the mantle area inside the **earth** out of which **igneous rocks** crystallize. Magma is not just molten rock, it also contains *volatiles*. These are substances which evaporate easily. They include **water**, **carbon dioxide**, hydrogen sulphide, **sulphur**, sulphur dioxide and **chlorine**. Water is by far the major volatile and may account for up to 8% of the magma.

magnet A magnet is a device which strongly attracts certain **metals** (**iron**, **steel**, nickel and cobalt) and affects an electric **current**).

Magnets are often made of iron or steel but may also be made of certain **alloys** or **ceramic** materials. *Electromagnets* have similar properties to magnets and are produced by the passage of an electric current.

The areas in a magnet where the attractive **force** appears to be concentrated are called the *poles*. The two poles are called north and south. The region around the magnet, in which there is a magnetic force, is called a **magnetic field**.

The *law of magnetic force* describes the behaviour of magnetic poles: like poles repel each other while unlike poles attract each other.

A *compass* is a small magnet which is used to establish direction relative to the earth's magnetic field. The earth behaves as if there is a magnetic south pole in the region of the geographic north pole. Hence, if a magnetic needle is suspended by a thread and allowed to swing freely, its north pole will point to geographic north. For this reason it is sometimes referred to as the north-seeking pole.

magnetic field A region of space around a **magnet** in which there is a magnetic **force**. Magnetic fields are three-dimensional but are usually represented as two-dimensional in draw ings. A magnetic field is shown as a series of imaginary magnetic field lines. The closeness of the field lines indicates their strength, while their direction is shown by arrow heads. Field lines are taken to run from north poles and to south poles.

(a) *Bar magnet*

(b) *U-magnet*

(c) *Two like poles*

(d) *A straight current*

(e) *A coil with current*

magnetic field Some simple magnetic fields.

mass A measure of the amount of matter in an object. It depends on the number of **molecules** it contains. The **SI unit** of mass is the kilogram, kg. The mass of an object does not vary with changes in **gravity** so an object would have the same mass of **earth** as on the **moon**

Mass should not be confused with **weight**, which changes with changes in gravity.

melting point The **temperature** at which a **solid** changes to a **liquid** (or a liquid to a solid). More precisely, it is the temperature at which solid and liquid forms of the same substance (e.g. ice/water) are in equilibrium. At constant **pressure** the melting point is constant for a pure substance, but it is lowered if impurities are added, hence ice melts when salt is sprinkled on it. The **energy** needed to cause melting without change of temperature is called **latent heat**.

menstrual cycle This is a reproductive cycle occurring in female primates (monkeys, apes and humans). The cycle is controlled by **hormones**. In human females, the cycle lasts about twenty-eight days. During this time the **uterus** wall thickens in preparation for implantation of a fertilized **ovum**. If fertilization does not occur the new uterus lining and the unfertilized ovum are expelled from the vagina. This part of the cycle is called *menstruation* and results in a small amount of bleeding from the vagina. See **fertilization** in humans, **ovulation**.

thickness of wall of uterus

oestrogen level in blood
causes repair of uterus wall

progesterone level in blood
prepares uterus for
implantation;

0 5   14   28 5   14   28
menstruation   menstruation
time in days

menstrual cycle

mercury The only **liquid metal** at room **temperatures**. It has many important uses. Here are some examples:

a) **Alloys** of mercury with other metals are called amalgams. Zinc amalgam is used for teeth fillings.

b) Mercury is used as the liquid in **thermometers**.

c) In mercury cells, the metal forms the cathode (negative **electrode**) in the **electrolysis** of sodium chloride solution to form sodium hydroxide.

Both mercury vapour and mercury compounds are poisonous and must be handled with extreme care.

metabolism A collective term describing all of the physical and chemical processes occurring within a living organism. These include both the synthesis (anabolism) and breakdown (catabolism) of **compounds**.

The rate of metabolism of a resting animal, measured by oxygen consumption, is known as the basal metabolic rate (BMR). It is the minimum amount of **energy** needed to maintain life and varies with species, age and gender.

metabolism

metal Many **elements** are metals. Pure metals are rarely used in modern life. Most metals are used in the form of **alloys**. Typical metals:
(a) Have a crystalline structure.
(b) Are strong and hard.
(c) Are malleable and ductile.
(d) Produce *cations* (positively charged ions).

(e) React with **acids**.

(f) React with **nonmetals**.

(g) Produce basic oxides.

(h) Good conductors of **heat** and electricity.

(i) Have high **melting** and **boiling points**.

metamorphic rocks Rocks which have re-crystallized, in the **solid** state, from existing rocks, in conditions of **heat** and **pressure**. This process is called *metamorphism*. It does not usually change the overall chemical composition of a rock but forms new minerals from those originally present. Metamorphic rocks form from **sedimentary rocks**, **igneous rocks** or other metamorphic rocks. See **rock cycle**.

Existing rock	→	Metamorphic rock
Sandstone		Quartzite
Limestone		Marble
Mudstone		Slate
Granite		Gneiss
Gneiss		Migmatite

methane A gaseous alkane with the formula CH_4. In the methane **molecule** the **hydrogen atoms** are arranged in the shape of a *tetrahedron* around the **carbon** atom.

Methane is the main constituent of **natural gas** and is also released from **petroleum**. It burns readily in a plentiful supply of **air** to give **carbon dioxide** and **water**, and is also an industrial source of hydrogen.

methane   A methane molecule.

microbe   A general term used to describe a microscopic organism (microorganism).

microscope   An optical instrument which gives a large image of a small object. In its simplest form a microscope consists of a single converging **lens**. Compound microscopes have two or more lenses. The lens nearest the object is called the *object lens* (objective) while the lens nearest the eye is called the *eye lens* (eyepiece).

microwaves   A region of the **spectrum** of **electromagnetic waves**. The approximate wavelength range is 1 mm to 10 m and the approximate **frequency** range is 10^7–10^{12} Hz. See **wave**.

Uses of microwaves include microwave cookers and **radar**. In microwave cookers the frequency used (typically 2450 MHz) is strongly absorbed by the food, causing it to heat up rapidly. The microwaves penetrate the food, which is cooked more quickly than in a conventional oven.

mineral salts Components of **soil** formed by the **weathering** of rocks and from **humus** mineralization. Mineral salts are found in solution in soil **water**. They are absorbed by plant roots and transported through the plant in solution. Like **vitamins**, mineral salts are needed in tiny amounts but are nevertheless vital for plant and, ultimately, animal nutrition. The absence of a particular mineral salt can lead to mineral deficiency, disease and death. Plants need at least twelve mineral salts for healthy growth.

(a) *Major elements* — needed in relatively large amounts: nitrogen, phosphorus, **sulphur**, potassium, **calcium**, magnesium.

(b) *Minor elements* — needed in very small amounts: manganese, **copper**, zinc, **iron**, boron, molybdenum. Some mineral salts are needed by plants, some are needed by animals, and some are needed by both. The properties of some important mineral salts are summarized on page 176.

mixture Two or more substances present in the same container, but not chemically bonded together (see **compound**). Some properties of mixtures:

(a) The proportions of substances in a mixture can vary.
(b) No **energy** is absorbed or released when a mixture is made.
(c) The **properties** of a mixture are the properties of all the components.
(d) Mixtures can be separated by physical methods.

Mineral salt	Function	Some deficiency effects
Calcium	Component of plant **cells** walls and animal **bones**.	Rickets in humans.
Iron	Component of haemoglobin.	Anaemia in humans.
Magnesium	Component of **chlorophyll**.	Pale yellow plant **leaves** (chlorosis).
Nitrogen	Component of **protein** and nucleic acids	Poor reproductive development in plants.
Phosphorus	Components of ATP, nucleic acids, cell membrane, animal bones.	Stunted plant growth

mineral salts

mole A mole is the **mass** of an **element** or **compound** which contains the same number of **atoms** or **molecules** as there are atoms in 12 g of **carbon**.

The mass of one mole of an element is the **rela-**

tive atomic mass (expressed in grams). The mass of one mole of a **compound** is the **relative molecular mass** (expressed in grams).

Symbol	H	C	O
Relative atomic masses	1	12	16
Mass of 1 mole of atoms	1 g	12 g	16 g
Formula	H_2	C	O_2
Mass of 1 mole of molecules	2 g	12 g	32 g

Thus the mass of 1 mole of water molecules is $2 \times 1 + 16 = 18$ g, and the mass of 1 mole of carbon dioxide molecules is $12 + 2 \times 16 = 44$ g.

molecular formula   The formula of a substance which shows the number and types of **atoms** found in the **molecule**. However, it does not tell us anything about the way in which those atoms are arranged (structure). For example, the molecular formula of water is H_2O, thus a molecule of water consists of two atoms of **hydrogen** and one atom of **oxygen**. It is not unusual for two substances with completely different structures and chemical properties to have the same molecular formula. For example, the chemicals butanol and ethoxyethane both have the molecular formula $C_4H_{10}O$. See **empirical formula**, **structural formula**.

molecule   This is the smallest particle of an **element** or **compound** which can exist independently. It contains two or more **atoms** bonded together in small whole numbers, e.g.

O_2	a molecule of **oxygen**
CH_4	a molecule of **methane**
$CaCO_3$	a molecule of calcium carbonate

moment The turning effect, or torque, of a **force**, or couple, around a point. The moment is given by the product of the force, F, and its perpendicular distance, s, from the turning point: T = Fs. The **SI unit** is the newton-metre. Nm.

Moments are often described as clockwise or anticlockwise, depending on the direction of the turning effect. The *law of moments* states that when an object is in equilibrium there is no net turning effect: the sum of the anticlockwise moments is equal to the sum of the clockwise moments.

moment In this example the anticlockwise moment and clockwise moment are both equal to 200 Nm.

momentum The momentum of an object is given by the product of its **mass** and **velocity**. The **SI unit** is the kilogram-metre per second, kgm/s. The *law of conservation of momentum* follows from **Newton's laws of motion**. It states that the total momentum of a group of objects remains constant unless a net outside force acts on them.

monomer The **compound** from which **polymers** are made. For example:

Monomer	Polymer
Chloroethene	Polychloroethene
Ethene	Polythene
Phenylethene	Polyphenylethene
(Styrene)	(Polystyrene)

moon A term used to describe a large natural satellite of any **planet**. It is, however, most often used when describing the earth's natural satellite. The moon is approximately 3460 km in diameter and 382 000 km from the earth.

The moon is a *non-luminous* source of light: it reflects light from the **sun**. As the moon revolves around the **earth** differing amounts are illuminated, giving rise to the 'phases of the moon'.
Half of the moon is illuminated at all times. The inner circle shows the position of the illuminated

moon The phases of the moon.

half of the moon. The outer circle shows how the moon looks from earth during its different phases. See **eclipse**.

The moon orbits the earth approximately once each month. See **tide**.

motor, electric A device which converts input electric **energy** into movement. In most electric motors movement is due to a central rotating coil. The structure of a simple motor is identical to that of a simple **generator**; however, they have opposite effects:

(a) In a generator the coil is turned and an electric **current** is produced in it.

b) In an electric motor an electric current passes through the coil and causes it to turn.

mucus A slimy **fluid** secreted by goblet **cells** found in the epithelia of vertebrates. Mucus has several important functions in humans.
a) It traps dust and **bacteria** in the air passages.
b) It lubricates the surfaces of the internal **organs**.
c) It lubricates the inside walls of the **alimentary canal**, making it possible for food to pass through easily.
d) The layer on the inside walls of the alimentary canal prevents digestive **enzymes** from reaching and digesting the walls themselves.

multicellular (of an organism) Consisting of many **cells**. Most animals and plants are multicellular. Compare **unicellular**.

muscle Animal **tissue** which consists of **cells** which are able to contract in response to nerve impulses, thus producing movement. This may be movement of internal **organs** within the animal or movement of the animal in its environment.

mutation A natural spontaneous change in the structure of **DNA** in **chromosomes**. Mutations are rare, but when they occur the resulting altered characteristic is passed on to subsequent

generations. Mutations most often confer dis
advantages on the organism inheriting them
however, mutations may also result in beneficia
variations within a *population*. Such beneficia
variations are the basis of **evolution**.

Mutations can be induced in organisms by
exposure to excessive **radiation**. The artificia
alteration of DNA in chromosomes is calle
genetic engineering. Scientists are currentl
looking at ways of using this technique t
improve the yield and immunity to disease o
many food crops.

National Grid   A network of cables, often sup
ported in the air by pylons, which connect the
country's power stations with **electricity** con
sumers. In general, electricity is generated i
power stations at 25 kV. It is transformed (se
transformer) to 275 or 400 kV for transmissio
over long distances through the National Grid
The **voltage** is reduced later by substation trans
formers to lower voltages suitable for domesti
(240 V) or industrial use.

natural frequency   The particular frequency a
which any system which can vibrate will vibrate
freely and naturally. The value of this depend
on the physical nature of the system. For exam
ple, a simple **pendulum** will swing at a

frequency which depends on its length and on the gravitational field strength at that place. The frequency of the note produced by blowing across the top of the bottle depends on the size and shape of the air space inside it. These examples of **resonance** are matched by others in electronics, radiation and nuclear physics.

natural gas A **mixture** containing mainly **hydrocarbon gases** which is found in deposits beneath the **earth's** surface. Natural gas and crude oil (see **petroleum**) are often found together. **Methane** is usually the major contituent and often makes up over 90% of the mixture. The **noble gas** helium is sometimes present in small amounts. Natural gas is used as a **fuel** in both industry and the home.

natural selection A theory first proposed by the famous scientist Charles Darwin to suggest how **evolution** could have taken place. Darwin suggested that individual organisms within a **species** differ in the extent to which they are adapted to conditions of their **environment**. Thus, in competition for food etc., the better-adapted organisms will survive and pass on their favourable **variations** to future generations. Conversely, the less well-adapted will die out.

nervous system A network of specialized **cells**

in **multicellular** animals. This network links receptors and effectors, thus coordinating the animal's activity. In mammals, the nervous system consists of the **brain** and the **spinal cord** (which together are called the central nervous system) and nerve cells connecting to all parts of the body.

neutralization A process where either the **pH** of an **acid** solution is increased to 7 or the **pH** of an alkaline solution is decreased to 7. pH 7 is neutral. An acid can be neutralized by adding a base or a **compound** such as a *carbonate*.

$$HCl(aq) + NaOH(aq) \rightarrow NaCl(aq) + H_2O(l)$$
$$2HCl(aq) + CuCO_3(s) \rightarrow CuCl_2(aq) + CO_2(g) + H_2O(l)$$

In acid-base reactions, **indicators** are used to show when the neutralization has occurred.

neutron One of the three main *subatomic particles* found in most **atoms**. The neutron has the same **mass** as a **proton** but carries no electrical **charge**.

Newton's laws of motion Three important statements which relate **forces** to each other and their effects on objects. They are valid for all forces and all cases, and form the basis of much physics:

First law: A body stays at rest, or if moving it

continues to move with uniform **velocity**, unless an external force acts on it making it behave differently.

Second law: The rate of change of **momentum** equals the net force. This is often written simply as; Force = **mass** × **acceleration** ($F = m \times a$).

Third law: When object A applies a force on object B, then B applies an equal but opposite force on A. This is often expressed as 'action and reaction are equal and opposite'.

The second law helps to define the newton, N, the unit of force. It is the force which will accelerate a mass of 1 kg by 1 m/s^2.

nitrogen cycle The circulation of the **element** *nitrogen* and its **compounds**. Much of this cycle is the result of metabolic processes (see **metabolism**) of living organisms. However, there are large amounts of synthetic nitrogen-containing **fertilizers** made from atmospheric nitrogen (via **ammonia** and nitric acid), used each year. These also play a significant part. Nitrates may also result from the action of lightning on atmospheric gases. See diagram on page 186.

noble gases or inert gases **Elements** in **group** 0 of the **periodic table**. They are all monatomic gases found in small amounts in the atmosphere,

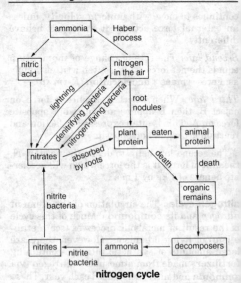

nitrogen cycle

i.e. helium, neon, argon, krypton, xenon.

Their electronic configurations are very stable because they have a complete outer shell of **electrons**. The elements do not easily lose or gain electrons. A few chemical **compounds** exist which contain **atoms** of the more massive noble gases (e.g. XeF_4) but these are man-made. When elements form **ions**, the electrons of these ions have an inert gas configuration, e.g.

Element	Ion	Electronic atom	configuration ion	Noble gas
Sodium	Na^+	2.8.1	2.8	Neon
Fluorine	F^-	2.7	2.8	Neon
Calcium	Ca^{2+}	2.8.8.2	2.8.8	Argon
Sulphur	S^{2-}	2.8.6	2.8.8	Argon
Aluminium	Al^{3+}	2.8.3	2.8	Neon
Bromine	Br^-	2.8.18.7	2.8.18.8	Krypton

nonmetals **Elements** which either:
(a) Have molecular structures and are **gases** at room temperature, or are **solids** or **liquids** with low **melting** and **boiling** points.
(b) Have **giant structures** with **covalent bonding**.

Typical nonmetals:
(a) Are poor conductors of heat and electricity.
(b) Give rise to *anions* (negatively charged ions).
(c) Do not react with **acids**.
(d) Produce acidic oxides.
(e) Form **covalent compounds**.

nuclear power The supply of useful **energy** from nuclear **fission** reactions in a *nuclear reactor*. The energy is produced by a controlled **chain reaction**. The **kinetic energy** of the particles produced by each fission produces a rise in

temperature. A coolant removes the **heat** energy to make steam. The steam drives turbines which, in turn, drive **generators**.

nucleus 1. The part within most **cells** which contains **chromosomes**. As the chromosomes contain the hereditary information, the nucleus controls the cell's activity through the action of the genetic material, **DNA**. The nuclear membrane isolates the nucleus from *cytoplasm*.

chromosome (DNA)

nucleus

nuclear membrane   cytoplasm

nucleus   Nucleus of a cell.

2. The part at the centre of an **atom** where the **mass** is concentrated. It contains **protons** and **neutrons**. The nucleus has a positive **charge**, and in the neutral atom this is balanced by negatively charged **electrons** moving around the nucleus. Atoms of the **isotope** hydrogen-1 are the only atoms whose nuclei contain no neutrons.

proton ———⊕⊕⊕—— neutron

nucleus   Nucleus of a lithium atom.

nylon The nylons are a group of *polyamide polymers*. The commonest of them is called nylon 6.6. See **polymerization**.

This synthetic *fibre* has great strength. It is used in fabrics, yarns (stockings, knitwear), carpets, ropes and nets. Nylon is useful because it will not rot, is hard-wearing and does not absorb **water**; however, it does stretch (useful in ropes and stockings).

Nylon is often mixed with other fibres such as wool to get a balance of properties. Generally speaking a nylon jumper is not as warm as a woollen one, however it will not wear out as quickly. A mixture of fibres produces a jumper which is both warm and hard-wearing.

oestrogen A **hormone** which is secreted by the **ovaries** of vertebrates. It stimulates the development of **secondary sexual characteristics** in female mammals, and plays an important role in the **menstrual cycle**.

oil A **liquid fat** such as melted butter, olive oil, sunflower oil, etc. The word is sometimes used in place of **petroleum**.

oleum A solution of sulphur(VI) oxide (sulphur trioxide) in concentrated **sulphuric acid**. Oleum is extremely corrosive and is a vigorous oxidizing agent, see **oxidation**.

optic nerve A cranial nerve found in vertebrates. It conducts nerve impulses from the retina of the **eye** to the **brain**.

orbit The closed path of an object moving in a central force field. For example, the **moon** travels in an orbit around the **earth** moving in the earth's gravitational field. The central force field is continually pulling the object towards it, thus preventing it from moving in a straight line. The object has both **potential** and **kinetic energy**.

ore A naturally occurring substance from which an **element** (often a **metal**) can be extracted. For example:

Ore	Element
galena	**lead**
haematite	**iron**
calomine	zinc
bauxite	**aluminium**
pitchblende	**uranium**

organ A collection of different **tissues** in a plant or animal which forms a structural and functional unit within an organism, such as the **leaf** of a plant or the **liver** of an animal. Different organs may be associated together to constitute a system; for example, the digestive system.

$$cells \rightarrow tissues \rightarrow organs \rightarrow systems$$

organic chemistry This branch of chemistry is concerned with the study of **compounds** of **carbon** but does not include carbonate hydrogen-carbonates, **carbon dioxide**, etc. Compare **inorganic chemistry**.

oscillator A **circuit** whose output is an **alternating current**. It is normal to be able to *tune* the **frequency** of the output by changing the value of a *capacitor* in the circuit. The active component in most oscillators is a *valve* or **transistor** which acts as an amplifier. Part of the output **energy** from the amplifier is fed back into the input to control the action. This is called **feedback**.

osmoregulation The control of the osmotic **pressure** and therefore the water content of an **organism** (see **osmosis**).

Freshwater fish gain water by osmosis and expel it as urine. Sea fish lose water by osmosis. They maintain water-balance by continual drinking and produce little urine.

In terrestrial organisms water is gained from food and drink and as a by-product of **respiration**. **Water** is lost during sweating, in exhaled air and as urine. The balance of water and **mineral salts** in the bodies of terrestrial animals

osmoregulation.   In seawater organisms.

osmoregulation   In freshwater organisms.

is mainly controlled by the **kidneys**.

osmosis   The **diffusion** of a solvent (usually **water**) through a selectively permeable membrane from a region of high solvent **concentration** to a region of lower solvent concentration. Examples of selectively permeable membranes are:

(a) The **cell** membrane.

(b) Visking (dialysis) tubing.

Selectively permeable membranes are thought to have tiny pores which allow the rapid passage of small water **molecules** but restrict the passage of larger solute molecules.

Since the cell membrane is selectively permeable, osmosis is important in the passage of water into and out of cells and organisms. The **pressure** exerted by the movement of water due to osmosis is called *osmotic pressure*.

osmosis Water passes through a selectively permeable membrane.

ovary 1. The hollow region in the **carpel** of a **flower** which contains one or more ovules. See **fertilization** in plants.

2. The reproductive **organ** of female animals. In vertebrates there are two ovaries. They produce **ova** and also release certain sex **hormones**. See **fertilization** in humans, **ovulation**.

ovulation A process which involves the release of an **ovum** onto the surface of a vertebrate **ovary**. From here it passes into the oviduct and then into the **uterus**.

In the human female, ovulation is controlled by **hormones** secreted by the pituitary gland. The sequence of events in the female's reproductive behaviour is called the **menstrual cycle**.

ovum An unfertilized female **gamete** produced at the **ovary** of many animals. An ovum contains a *haploid* **nucleus**. See **fertilization**, **ovulation**.

oxidation A substance is oxidized if it:
(a) Gains **oxygen**, e.g.

$$2Mg(s) + O_2(g) \rightarrow 2MgO(s)$$
magnesium   oxygen   magnesium oxide

(b) Loses **hydrogen**, e.g.

$$CH_4(g) + Cl_2(g) \rightarrow CH_3Cl(l) + HCl(g)$$
methane   chlorine   chloromethane   hydrogen chloride

) Loses **electrons**, e.g.

$$Cu(s) \rightarrow Cu^{2+}(aq) + 2e^-$$

copper   copper ions   electrons

A substance which brings about the oxidation of another substance is called an oxidizing agent. Compare **reduction**.

oxygen (O_2) A gaseous nonmetallic **element** in **group** VI of the **periodic table**. The **gas** is both colourless and odourless and makes up 21% of the **atmosphere**. It is vital for the **respiration** of both plants and animals. Although atmospheric oxygen is used up during respiration the supply is continually replenished by plants as a result of **photosynthesis**. Oxygen is only slightly soluble in **water**; however, there is normally enough dissolved to support fish and other aquatic life. **Pollution** often causes a drop in the **concentration** of oxygen in the water to such an extent that fish will suffocate and die. Oxygen is obtained industrially by the *fractional distillation* of liquefied **air**. In the laboratory it is obtained by the decomposition of hydrogen peroxide, usually with the help of a **catalyst** such as manganese(IV) oxide.

$$2H_2O_2(aq) \rightarrow 2H_2O(l) + O_2(g)$$

The chemical test for oxygen is to put a glowing splint into the gas. If the gas is oxygen the splint will relight. Oxygen will also make anythin, already burning in air burn much more fiercely.

Oxygen is a vigorous *oxidizing agent*. It is use extensively in **steel**-making and welding, as rocket propellant together with kerosine o **hydrogen**, and for life-support systems i medicine.

ozone layer   A region of the **atmosphere** abou 30 km above the **earth**'s surface, which is rich i ozone. (The **gas** ozone is an allotrope of **oxyge** where the **molecule** is triatomic (O_3).) This laye prevents most **ultraviolet radiation** from reach ing the earth. This is important, as exposure t excess ultraviolet radiation is known to caus skin cancer.

Scientists have recently become aware of hole appearing in the ozone layer allowing unusuall large amounts of ultraviolet radiation to reac the earth. Chemicals called *chlorofluorocarbon* (*CFCs*), used as aerosol propellants and in man industrial processes, are thought to be the caus Some CFCs eventually diffuse up into the ozon layer. They are very unreactive chemicals unde normal room conditions; however, in th presence of sunlight they react with the ozon thus destroying it. Steps are now being taken t reduce the amounts of CFCs used in the world.

pacemaker   A region of the *vertebrate* **hear**

where the contraction at each **heartbeat** starts. This word is often used to refer to an electronic device which may be inserted into the chest of a person suffering from certain types of heart disease. The device provides the heart with the electrical impulses needed for a regular beat.

pancreas A gland situated near the duodenum (see **alimentary canal**) of vertebrates. It releases an alkaline fluid containing digestive **enzymes** such as lipase, amylase and trypsin into the duodenum (see **digestion**). The pancreas also contains **tissue** known as the *Islets of Langerhans* which secretes the **hormone insulin**, which is important in the **metabolism** of **sucrose**.

parasite An organism that feeds in or on another living organism called the *host*. In a parasitic relationship the host does not benefit and may actually be harmed. Examples in man include fleas, lice and tapeworms.

particle (In physics) an object whose **volume** is very small. The **kinetic model** describes the structure of matter in terms of particles. In simple pictures of matter, such particles are called **atoms** or **molecules**. Studies have revealed that particles can sometimes appear as **waves** because they can show wave properties like **diffraction** and interference.

pascal (Pa) The **SI unit** of pressure. 1 pascal = 1 newton/metre².

pendulum A regularly swinging object with a regular transfer to and fro between **potential** and **kinetic energy**.

The period of a pendulum is the time it takes to complete one full cycle.

The value of the period, T, depends only on the length, *l*, of the pendulum and the acceleration due to gravity, *g*. The value of *g* can be estimated by carrying out a simple experiment with a pendulum and putting the results into the following equation.

$$g = \frac{4 \times \pi^2 \times l}{T^2}$$

	A	B	C
potential energy	yes	no	yes
kinetic energy	no	yes	no

pendulum The period of this pendulum is the time it takes to swing from A to C and back to A.

periodic table A table representing all of the **elements** so as to show similarities and differences in their chemical properties. (See page 200).

The elements are arranged in increasing order of **atomic number (Z)** as you read from left to right across the table. The horizontal rows are called *periods* and the vertical columns are called **groups**. There is a progression from **metals** to **nonmetals** across the period. This is period 3:

element	Na	Mg	Al	Si	P	S	Cl	Ar
atomic number	11	12	13	14	15	16	17	18
	metals					nonmetals		

This is part of group I;

Li
Na
K

The block of elements between Groups II and III are called *transition metals*. The chemistry of these metals is similar in many ways. Elements 58–71 are known as the *Lanthanide* or *Rare Earth* elements. Elements 90–103 are known as the *Actinide* elements. The elements which have atomic numbers greater than 92 do not occur naturally but have been made artificially by bombarding other elements with **particles**.

pest A general term used to describe any organism which is considered to have a

periodic table

Key:
- Symbol: H
- Atomic number: 1

Group I	II					transition elements						III	IV	V	VI	VII	0
H 1																	He 2
Li 3	Be 4											B 5	C 6	N 7	O 8	F 9	Ne 10
Na 11	Mg 12											Al 13	Si 14	P 15	S 16	Cl 17	Ar 18
K 19	Ca 20	Sc 21	Ti 22	V 23	Cr 24	Mn 25	Fe 26	Co 27	Ni 28	Cu 29	Zn 30	Ga 31	Ge 32	As 33	Se 34	Br 35	Kr 36
Rb 37	Sr 38	Y 39	Zr 40	Nb 41	Mo 42	Tc 43	Ru 44	Rh 45	Pd 46	Ag 47	Cd 48	In 49	Sn 50	Sb 51	Te 52	I 53	Xe 54
Cs 55	Ba 56	La 57	Hf 72	Ta 73	W 74	Re 75	Os 76	Ir 77	Pt 78	Au 79	Hg 80	Tl 81	Pb 82	Bi 83	Po 84	At 85	Rn 86
Fr 87	Ra 88	Ac 89	*Unq 104	*Unp 105													

Ce 58	Pr 59	Nd 60	Pm 61	Sm 62	Eu 63	Gd 64	Tb 65	Dy 66	Ho 67	Er 68	Tm 69	Yb 70	Lu 71
Th 90	Pa 91	U 92	Np 93	Pu 94	Am 95	Cm 96	Bk 97	Cf 98	Es 99	Fm 100	Md 101	No 102	Lr 103

detrimental effect on humans. This effect may be to the body, to the food supply or to the **environment**. Some examples are shown in the following table.

Example of pest	Effect on humans
weeds; locusts	Reduces the **growth** of plants and crops.
foot and mouth virus	Causes disease in domestic animals
woodworm, wet rot fungus	Damages buildings
mosquito; lice	Transmits human disease.

Methods used to combat pests include:
(a) Spraying with chemical **pesticides**.
(b) Using natural **predators** against the pest.
(c) Introducing **parasites** and disease-bearing organisms to the pest population.
(d) Introducing sterile (unable to breed) individuals to the pest population, thus reducing the reproductive capacity.

pesticide A chemical **compound**, often delivered as a spray or fine powder, which kills or prevents the **growth** of pests which damage crops. Pesticides are often divided into three groups:
(a) *Herbicides*. Chemicals which act on plants (weedkillers), e.g. paraquat.
(b) *Fungicides*. Chemicals which act on fungal

growths, e.g. Cheshunt compound.

(c) *Insecticides*. Chemicals which act on insects, e.g. DDT (now banned in Britain).

Pesticides are used to increase the yield of crops, however there are certain disadvantages associated with their use:

(a) They may kill organisms other than the target pest.

(b) The **concentration** of pesticide increases as it passes through a **food chain**.

(c) Some pesticides decompose very slowly and may accumulate into harmful doses within consumer organisms.

(d) By killing off susceptible organisms, they allow resistant individuals to grow and multiply with reduced competition.

petroleum The **mixture** of **hydrocarbons**, e.g. **natural gas** and *crude oil*, found in the earth's crust. It is thought to have been produced over millions of years by the action of **heat** and **pressure** on the remains of marine animals and plant organisms.

There are large reserves of petroleum in the Middle East, United States, Soviet Union, Central America and North Sea. Petroleum is the raw material of the petrochemical industry and is the source of petrol, diesel fuel, heating oil, fuel oil and gas supplies. These products are obtained by the *fractional distillation* of

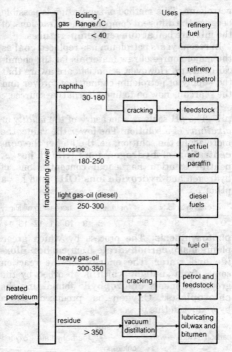

petroleum Fractional distillation

petroleum. This method of separation is possible because the different components, or fractions, of the mixture boil at different **temperatures**.

In recent years petroleum has replaced **coal** as the major source of raw materials for the chemical industry. However, scientists are aware that the supply of petroleum cannot last forever and the search is now on to find alternative sources.

pH The pH scale is a measure of the *acidity* or *alkalinity* of a solution. The lower the value, the more acidic the solution, i.e. the higher the **concentration** of **hydrogen ions** (H^+) it has. A neutral solution has equal concentrations of hydrogen and **hydroxide ions** (OH^-) and has a pH of 7.

increasing acidity						neutral				increasing alkalinity			
0	1	2	3	4	5	6	7	8	9	10	11	12	13	14

photosynthesis The process by which green plants make **carbohydrate** from **carbon dioxide** and **water**. The **energy** for the reaction comes from sunlight which is absorbed by the green pigment **chlorophyll** found in the **chloroplasts**. **Oxygen** is produced as a byproduct in this process.

$$\text{carbon dioxide} + \text{water} \xrightarrow[\text{chlorophyll}]{\text{light energy}} \text{carbohydrate} + \text{oxygen}$$

$$6CO_2 \qquad 6H_2O \qquad\qquad C_6H_{12}O_6 \ + \ 6O_2$$

Photosynthesis is the source of all food and the basis of **food chains**, while the release of oxygen replenishes the oxygen content of the **atmosphere**. The process is thus essential to the functioning of the **biosphere**.

physical change A change to a substance which involves changes in its physical properties, e.g. **temperature**, particle size, state, etc., but no alteration to its chemical properties. Compare **chemical change**.

placenta An organ which develops in the **uterus** of a female mammal during **pregnancy**. It allows a close association between the blood circulation of the mother and that of the **foetus**. The placenta allows the passage of food and **oxygen** from the mother to the foetus and the removal of the waste products **carbon dioxide** and **urea** from the foetus.

planet One of nine known members of the **solar system** which revolve around the **sun**. See Appendix F.

plankton The collective word used for microscopic animals and plants which float in the surface waters of lakes and seas. Plankton play a vital role as the starting point of aquatic **food chains**.

plasma The clear fluid of vertebrate blood in which the blood cells are suspended. It is an aqueous solution containing many dissolved **compounds** which are transported to different parts of the body, e.g.

(a) Waste products: **carbon dioxide**, **urea**;
(b) Digested foods: **glucose**, **amino acids**;
(c) **hormones**, **plasma proteins**, **sodium chloride**.

plastic 1. The nature of an object when it has been deformed beyond its *elastic limit*. Compare **elasticity**.
  2. A substance which can be formed into a desired shape very easily. See **thermoplastic**, **thermosetting plastic**.

polarization Restricting the vibrations during transverse **wave** motion to a single plane. During transverse wave motion, the *vibration* is perpendicular to the direction in which the wave is travelling. There are many different directions in which this can occur.
Like all **electromagnetic waves**, **light** can be polarized. Some sunglasses polarize light passing through them, reducing glare. Some *minerals* are characteristic colours under polarized light and this is used to identify them.

pollen The reproductive spores of flowering plants. Each pollen grain contains a male

gamete. Pollen grains may be transferred either by insects or by the wind, and they are adapted to their particular mode of transfer.
See **fertilization in plants, pollination**.

(a) spiky and sticky   (b) smooth and light

air bladders

pollen Pollen grains adapted to (a) Insect pollination. (b) Wind pollination.

pollination The transfer of **pollen** grains from the **stamens** (male part of a **flower**) to **carpels** (female part of a flower) in flowering plants.

(a) *Self-pollination* involves the transfer of pollen within the same flower or between flowers on the same plant.

(b) *Cross-pollination* involves the transfer of pollen between two separate plants.

Normally the male and female parts of a plant do not mature at the same time, so cross-pollination is more likely. This results in the mixing of **chromosomes** and may lead to **variation**. Pollen is transferred either by the wind or on the bodies of insects. Flowers are adapted to favour one particular method of pollen transfer.

(a) *Insect pollination* — the flowers are generally highly coloured and/or scented and contain nectar. Insects are attracted by the colour and scent and visit the flower to collect the nectar. Their bodies become dusted with pollen. Some of this pollen may stick to the stigmas of subsequent flowers which they visit.

(b) *Wind pollination* — the flowers are often drab and have no scent. They produce many more pollen grains than insect-pollinated plants, as much of the pollen is lost in transfer. See **fertilization in plants, flowers, pollen**.

pollution A general word for the addition of any substance to an **environment** which upsets the natural balance. Pollution has resulted mainly from *industrialization*. Two important factors have been a large increase in the **combustion** of **fossil fuels** and a migration of people from the land to towns and cities. Pollution of the **air** and **water** are often singled out as particularly important (see **biosphere**).

(a) Air pollution is caused mainly by the combustion of fossil fuels.

coal → smoke + **carbon dioxide** + sulphur dioxide

petrol → smoke + carbon + nitrogen + **lead**
                              monoxide   oxides

Air pollutants such as smoke and sulphur dioxide cause irritation to the human respiratory system and may accelerate diseases such as bronchitis and lung cancer. Sulphur dioxide and nitrogen oxides are responsible for **acid rain**. Lead is thought to retard the mental development of children.

b) Water pollution is caused by the intentional or accidental addition of materials into both freshwater and seawater. Most pollutants originate from industrial and agricultural practices and from the home. For example, mine and quarry washings, **acids, pesticides, fertilizers**, oil, radioactive discharges, detergents, hot water (from power stations). Some pollutants, such as pesticides, may poison and kill aquatic organisms. Other pollutants, such as sewage, cause an increase in the population of microorganisms in the water. The result is a reduction in the dissolved oxygen level, making it impossible for other organisms to survive. This process is called *eutrophication*.

polymers Large **molecules** in which a group of **atoms** is repeated; e.g.

$$x-x-x-x-x-x-x-x$$
$$\text{or}$$
$$x-y-x-y-x-y-x-y$$

Polymers may be naturally occurring substances

such as **starch** and **cellulose**, or synthetic substances such as **nylon** and *polythene*. See **polymerization**.

polymerization Any process in which small **molecules** (**monomers**) combine together to form large molecules (**polymers**).

Addition polymerization involves one kind of molecule containing a carbon-carbon double bond. **Electrons** are transferred from the double bonds allowing the molecules to join together to form a long chain of carbon-carbon single bonds. See diagram opposite.

Condensation polymerization involves two kinds of molecule which condense together to form long chains. A small molecule is lost during the reaction. This is often, but not always, **water**. See diagram on page 212.

potential energy The **energy** which an object has stored up because of its position. For example, **water** at the top of a waterfall has potential energy. As the water drops, the potential energy changes into **kinetic energy**. Potential energy can also be stored as elastic, chemical or electrical energy.

potential difference See **voltage**.

power (P) The rate of **energy** transfer or the

ethene   polythene

polymerization   Polythene.

polymerization Nylon.

rate of working. The unit, the **watt**, is the transfer of one **joule** per second. The horsepower was once used as a unit of power; one horsepower is equivalent to just under 750 watts. Here are some useful equations involving power.

$$\text{mechanical power} = \textbf{force} \times \textbf{velocity} = \frac{\text{work done}}{\text{time taken}} = Fv$$

$$\text{electrical power} = \textbf{voltage} \times \textbf{current} = VI$$

Efficiency is often expressed in terms of power.

$$\text{efficiency} = \frac{\text{useful output power}}{\text{total input power}}$$

In the case of a **transformer**;

$$\text{efficiency} = \frac{P_2}{P_1} = \frac{V_2 \times I_2}{V_1 \times I_1}$$

precipitate (ppt) The insoluble substance formed when two solutions are mixed in a double decomposition reaction. In each of the following examples the precipitate is <u>underlined</u> and appears as a **solid** when the two clear solutions are mixed.

$$Pb(NO_3)_2(aq) + 2NaCl(aq) \rightarrow \underline{PbCl_2}(s) + 2NaNO_3(aq)$$

| lead(II) nitrate | sodium chloride | <u>lead(II) chloride</u> | sodium nitrate |

$$BaCl_2(aq) + Na_2SO_4(aq) \rightarrow \underline{BaSO_4}(s) + 2NaCl(aq)$$

| barium chloride | sodium sulphate | <u>barium sulphate</u> | sodium chloride |

predator An animal which feeds on other animals which are called the *prey*. A predator is a food consumer but not a **parasite**. The relationship between predator and prey is reflected in their numbers. The numbers of predators and prey in an area may follow a cycle.

We can interpret the cycle as follows:
(a) When prey is plentiful a larger number of predators will survive as there is less competition for food.
(b) More predators will eat more prey, so the number of prey will decline.
(c) Fewer prey enable fewer predators to survive as there is now more competition for food.
(d) Fewer predators will eat fewer prey, so the number of prey will increase.

predator   The predator/prey cycle.

pregnancy or **gestation period** The time between conception and birth in mammals. Human pregnancy lasts for approximately forty weeks and during this time the **embryo**, which has become implanted in the **uterus**, develops. In the early stages of pregnancy, finger-like structures (called *villi*) grow from the embryo into the uterus wall and develop into the **placenta**. This allows the transfer of **oxygen** and food from the mother to the embryo and the removal of **carbon dioxide** and **urea**. During the pregnancy the

pregnancy (a) Implanted embryo. (b) Relationship between uterus and placenta.

pregnancy (a) Human foetus after twenty weeks. (b) Human foetus just before birth.

cells of the embryo continually divide and differentiate. The growing embryo (now called a **foetus**) becomes suspended in a water-filled sac called the *amnion*. The placenta extends into the umbilical cord which connects with the abdomen of the foetus.

pressure (*p*) The **force** on a unit area of a surface from the substance in contact with it. The unit of pressure is the **pascal** (Pa) (1 Pa = 1 N/m²). To calculate pressure we use the equation; pressure (Pa) = force (N)/area (m²). Often the force applied to an object is **weight** *W*.

The pressure at a depth in a **liquid** or in the **air** equals the weight above the unit area. This gives the relationship; pressure = depth × mean **density** × *g*. The pressure exerted by the air is called *atmospheric pressure*. Pressure may be measured by a variety of instruments, e.g. manometer, Bourdon gauge, **barometer**.

primary sexual characteristics The features which distinguish between males and females from the time of their birth. Primary sexual characteristics do not include those which develop at puberty and are characteristic of adulthood. Compare **secondary**, **sexual characteristics**.

progesterone A **hormone** secreted by the

ovaries of a mammal. It prepares the **uterus** to receive the fertilized embryo and prevents any further **ovulation** during the **pregnancy**.

properties The characteristic ways in which a substance behaves (reacts) that make it what it is and make it different from other substances. Properties are often classified as *physical* or *chemical*. Chemical properties relate to the chemical reactions of the substance.

Chemical properties include whether the substance:	Physical properties include:
is a **metal** or **nonmetal**;	colour
gives acidic or basic oxides;	density
has more than one **valency**;	physical state
reacts with **acids**;	boiling point
is an oxidizing or reducing	melting point
agent	solubility

proteins Organic **compounds** containing the elements **carbon**, **hydrogen**, **oxygen**, nitrogen and sometimes **sulphur**. A simple **molecule** of protein consists of a long chain of subunits called **amino acids**. These chains may be joined to other chains and folded in several different ways, resulting in very large and complex molecules.

Proteins are the building blocks of **cells** and **tissues**, being important constituents of **muscle**, **skin**, **bone**, etc. Proteins also play a vital role as

enzymes, and some **hormones** also have a protein structure.

proton A positively charged subatomic **particle** found in the **nucleus** of the **atom**. The number of protons in an atom is given by the **atomic number**. **Isotopes** of any **element** always contain the same number of protons.

pulley A type of machine which transfers an applied **force** by means of the *tension* in a rope, cable or chain. One or more pulley wheels change the direction and/or the size of the applied force. Pulleys are often assumed to be 100% efficient (see **efficiency**) for the purpose of calculations. However, some **energy** is 'wasted' due to **friction** in the pulley bearings and stretching of the rope or cable.

pulley   Three examples.

pulse rate The regular beating of blood in **arteries** due to the **heartbeat**. Pulse rate can be detected in the human body where an artery runs close to the **skin**. The wrist is often used for taking someone's pulse. In an adult human, pulse rate varies between about 70 beats per minute at rest to over 100 beats per minute during exercise.

radar A technique for finding the direction and distance of an object by analysing its **reflection** of **microwaves**.

Pulses of waves are emitted in different directions. Waves which hit objects are reflected back to a detector. The direction from which the waves are reflected gives the direction of the object. From knowing the speed of the microwaves, and the time taken to reach the object and be reflected back to the detector, it is possible to calculate the distance to the object.

If the object is moving there is a **frequency** change during reflection; this is called the *Doppler effect*. The size of the frequency change gives the object's speed. This method is used by traffic police to measure the speed of vehicles.

radiation The transfer of **energy** by either **waves** or particles. Any radiating object therefore loses energy. **Heat** radiation is energy transfer by **infrared** waves. It leaves all objects at a rate that depends on **temperature**, however, black surfaces radiate (and absorb) these waves better than white ones unless the temperature is very high. Cosmic radiation consists of a stream of very fast particles. The source of cosmic radiation is not known for certain, but is thought to be exploding **stars**. See **electromagnetic waves**, **radioactivity**, **sound**.

radio   A region of the **spectrum** of **electromagnetic waves**. The approximate wavelength range is 10–10^6 m and the approximate **frequency** range is 10^2–10^7 Hz. The most important use of radio is in telecommunications. The following table lists the main bands used.

Band	Wavelength range/m
LF low frequency	10^4–10^3
MF medium frequency	10^3–10^2
HF high frequency	10^2–10
VHF very high frequency	10 –1
UHF ultra-high frequency	1 –0.1

Part of the VHF and UHF bands are in the **microwave** region of the electromagnetic spectrum; however, they are often included with radio as they are also used for telecommunication.

Radio communication is helped by the *ionosphere*. This is a region of the upper **atmo-**

sphere, from about 40–400 km above the ground. Many of the **air particles** in the ionosphere are ionized (hence the name), mainly by **ultraviolet radiation** from the **sun**. The ionized layer reflects the radio waves.

Radio waves which have wavelengths of less

radio Radio waves are reflected by the ionosphere.

radio Television programmes have to be reflected by satellite.

than 10 m are used to carry television programmes. Unfortunately these are not reflected by the ionosphere, and communication of live television programmes across the world depends on reflection from suitably placed satellites.

radioactivity The decay (breakdown) of unstable **nuclei** into more stable forms. During the **decay energy** is transferred to the products; they move away; they have **kinetic energy**. There are several forms of radioactivity.

(a) Alpha decay involves the release of **alpha particles**. The alpha particle, α, is a helium nucleus and has a **mass** of four units. When a parent nucleus, X, changes to a daughter nucleus, Y, the mass of Y is four units less than that of X and its **proton** number is two less.

(b) There are several forms of beta decay. In the most common, a **neutron** in the parent nucleus changes to a proton and an **electron beta particle**, β, escapes.

(c) **Gamma radiation**, γ, is the result of a simple change of energy structure in the nucleus.

(d) In the case of **fission**, the parent nucleus splits into two smaller daughters with the release of a few neutrons. A **chain reaction** may occur.

(e) A few radioactive nuclei become more stable by the release of protons.

In all cases the daughter nuclei may themselves be radioactive, and may produce a different form of radioactivity from the parent nucleus. For this reason it is difficult to provide a pure source of any one form of radioactive **radiation**. See **half-life**.

rain gauge   A device for measuring the amount of rain over a given period of time (often 24 hours).

rate of reaction   The rate (or **speed**) at which a chemical reaction proceeds. This depends on several factors:

(a) **Temperature**. The higher the temperature, the faster the reaction, because the **particles** are moving with greater **energies**.

(b) *Particle size*. The smaller the particles involved, the greater the total surface area available for reaction, hence the faster the reaction.

(c) **Concentration**. The more concentrated a solution (or the higher the **pressure** of a **gas**) the more particles there are in a given **volume**. The more particles are available for reaction, the faster the reaction will be.

(d) **Catalysts**. These change the rate by providing an alternative reaction pathway along which the reaction can proceed.

reactivity series A series of **elements** arranged in order of their chemical reactivity. For example, the following series shows a group of metals in order of decreasing activity.

> Potassium
> **Sodium**
> **Calcium**
> Magnesium
> **Aluminium**
> Zinc
> **Iron**
> **Lead**
> **Copper**
> Silver

The position in the series indicates the reactivity of an element in chemical reactions. For example, potassium reacts violently with **water**, magnesium reacts very slowly with water but more vigorously with steam. Copper reacts with neither water nor steam. See **electrochemical series**.

rectifier A device which allows **current** in only one direction. Most forms are types of **diodes**. Rectifiers are used to convert **alternating current** into **direct current**.

A smoothing capacitor makes the signal more steady, however the output may still not be steady enough for all uses.

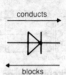

rectifier Current flows in one direction only.

rectifier The effect of rectification on alternating current.

rectifier A **circuit** showing a simple rectifier of the type used in power packs for toy trains and in microcomputers.

red blood cell or **red blood corpuscle** or **erythrocyte** The most numerous **cell** in vertebrate **blood**. Red blood cells are responsible for transporting **oxygen** from the **lungs** to the **tissues** of the body. In humans, they are biconcave discs and are made in the **bone** marrow. When formed, a red blood cell has a **nucleus**; however, this is lost by the time the cell enters the blood.

diameter
eight microns   side

red blood cell

Red blood cells contain haemoglobin. When blood passes through the lungs, haemoglobin combines with oxygen to form the unstable **compound** oxyhaemoglobin. At the tissues this compound breaks down, releasing oxygen to the cells.

$$\text{haemoglobin} + \text{oxygen} \underset{\text{tissues}}{\overset{\text{lungs}}{\rightleftharpoons}} \text{oxyhaemoglobin}$$

A shortage of red blood cells is called anaemia. Compare **white blood cell**.

reduction A substance is reduced if it:

(a) Loses oxygen, e.g.

$$\underset{\text{lead oxide}}{PbO(s)} + \underset{\text{carbon}}{C(s)} \rightarrow \underset{\text{lead}}{Pb(s)} + \underset{\text{carbon monoxide}}{CO(g)}$$

(b) Gains **hydrogen**, e.g.

$$\underset{\text{chlorine}}{Cl_2(g)} + \underset{\text{hydrogen}}{H_2(g)} \rightarrow \underset{\text{hydrogen chloride}}{2HCl(g)}$$

(c) Gains **electrons**, e.g.

$$\underset{\text{sodium ion}}{Na^+(l)} + \underset{\text{electron}}{e^-} \rightarrow \underset{\text{sodium}}{Na(l)}$$

A substance which brings about the reduction of another substance is called a reducing agent. There are several common reducing agents:

Hydrogen	H_2
Carbon	C
Carbon monoxide	CO
Sulphur dioxide	SO_2
Hydrogen sulphide	H_2S

Compare **oxidation**.

refining A process which involves either the removal of impurities from a substance or the extraction of a substance from an impure **mixture**.

reflection One of the three things which can happen to **radiation** is one medium when it meets the surface of a second medium (see **absorption**, **refraction**). Reflected radiation bounces back into the first medium.

The two laws of reflection allow us to predict where a given *incident ray* will go after reflection at a given point, the *point of incidence*. Angles are measured from the *normal*. This is the perpendicular to the surface at the point of incidence.

(a) The reflected ray is in the same plane as the incident ray and the normal.

(b) The angle of reflection, r, equals the angle of incidence, i.

reflex action Reflex action occurs in most animals and in vertebrates. It is a rapid response to a **stimulus** over which the animal has no control. Reflex actions can be important in protecting animals from injury; e.g. withdrawing a hand from a hot object.

The *nerve impulse* responsible for reflex actions constitutes a *reflex arc* which is set up when a nerve impulse is initiated in the receptor. The impulse is transmitted along a *sensory neurone* to the **spinal cord** where it crosses a *synapse* to a *motor neurone*. This pathway enables the response to be very rapid.

When a reflex arc operates, nerve impulses are

also sent from the spinal cord to the **brain**. Thus, although the response is initiated by the spinal cord, it is through the brain that the animal is aware of what has happened. See **nervous system**.

reflex action

refraction One of three things which can happen to **radiation** in one medium when it meets the surface of a second (see **absorption, reflection**). After refraction the radiation travels on through the second medium, almost always in a different direction. If the direction is not different, the radiation has not been refracted. The two laws of refraction allow us to predict where a given *incident ray* will go after refraction at a point, the *point of incidence*. Angles are measured from the *normal* or *perpendicular* to the surface at the point of incidence.

(a) The *refracted ray* is in the same plane as the incident ray and the normal.

(b) For a given pair of media, the sine of the angle of incidence (i) divided by the sine of the angle of refraction (r) is constant (Snell's law).

This constant is the *refractive index* (n). It relates to the **speeds** of the radiation in the two media (see also **colour, lens**). When **light** passes from a less dense medium to a more dense medium it is refracted towards the normal in the more dense medium.

refraction   Refraction of light from a less dense medium to a more dense medium.

This is caused by the change of speed of the light. When light passes from a more dense medium to a less dense medium the converse is true. When light from a submerged object passes from water to air it is refracted. This causes the object to appear less deep than it really is.

Water waves are refracted when passing from water of one depth to water of a different depth.

refraction Refraction of light passing from water to air.

refraction Refraction of water waves at a change in depth, as a result of the change in speed.

refrigeration A method for transferring **energy** from a cool box to the warmer outside **air**. This is the opposite direction to normal net energy transfer and is achieved by a pump powered by a **motor**. The pump circulates a special **fluid** around a closed loop.

When the pump raises the fluid's **pressure** it becomes a **liquid** and gives off **latent heat**. At this stage the liquid goes through the black radiator coil outside so that heat can be transferred to the air. Further around the loop the liquid is forced through the valve to the low pressure side of the loop. The lower pressure causes the liquid to evaporate, absorbing latent heat from the surroundings. At this stage the substance is within the cool box. Devices like this which transfer heat from one place to another are often called *heat pumps*.

relative atomic mass (RAM) The average **mass** of the **atoms** of an **element** compared with an atom of the **isotope carbon**-12 which is given the value of exactly 12. See **relative molecular mass**.

relative molecular mass (RMM) The **mass** of one molecule of a **compound** calculated by adding together the **relative atomic mass** of each **atom** within the molecule. For example:

RMM of **carbon dioxide** (CO_2) = $12 + 2 \times 16 = 44$
RMM of **ammonia** (NH_3) = $14 + 3 \times 1 = 17$

relay An electrical device which allows a small **current** to control a large one.
When a current passes through the coil of an **electromagnet** the core attracts the iron armature. As it turns on the pivot it closes the

contacts, completing the main circuit. If the coil is switched off, the armature returns to its original position and the main circuit is broken.

relay

renewable energy sources A general term for sources of **energy** which are renewed by natural processes. For example, a fast-flowing river is a renewable energy source. The **water** in it can be used to drive **generators** thus producing electricity (**hydroelectricity**). After driving the generators the water eventually flows out to sea. Some of it will evaporate into the air and return onto the land as rain. Thus it will drain into the rivers ready to be used again. Other examples of renewable energy sources are **geothermal aquifers**, **geothermal hot dry rock structures**, **landfill gas**, **solar cells**, **wave generators** and **wind turbines**.

resistance (*R*) The opposition of a **circuit** element or section to the flow of **charge** (**current**, I). The unit of resistance is the ohm. The current I in a **metal** sample at a constant **temperature** is proportional to the **voltage**, V across its ends: $I \propto V$ (*Ohm's Law*). We define the sample's resistance R from this. $R = V/I$ (rearranging this equation $V = I \times R$, $I = V/R$). All normal circuit components have resistance. As they oppose current there is energy transfer producing a **temperature** rise (see **fuse**). The **power**, P, involved is the rate of energy transfer; it is given by:

$$P = V \times I \quad (= V^2/R \text{ or } I^2 \times R)$$

Temperature often alters a sample's resistance. In most metals, the increase in temperature makes R rise. In semiconductors, carbon and insulators, R falls. *Resistors* may be arranged in *series* or in *parallel* in a circuit.

When arranged in series the total resistance, R, of the group is given by;

$$R = R_1 + R_2 + R_3$$

When arranged in parallel the total resistance, R, of the group is given by:

$$\frac{1}{R} = \frac{1}{R_1} + \frac{1}{R_2} + \frac{1}{R_3}$$

resonance The large amplitude vibration of a system when it is driven at a **frequency** close to its **natural frequency**. Here are some examples of resonance:

(a) If one sings a note near a piano some of the strings will start to vibrate in sympathy.

(b) The tuning circuit of a radio set will pass high-amplitude signals only if their frequency is near its natural value.

(c) Resonance between the wind and the Tacoma Narrows Bridge (USA) caused the bridge to shake itself apart in 1940.

resources The products which are available within an area. The resources of an area may be described in many different ways. For example:

(a) The amount of food which can be grown.

(b) The mineral deposits which are present.

(c) The **energy** sources it has in the form of **coal**, **oil**, **natural gas**, **petroleum**, etc.

See **resource scarcity**.

resource scarcity Many **resources** are nonrenewable, they can only be used once. For example, **coal** is a nonrenewable energy source. Once burnt it cannot be used a second time. Much of the **metal** which is obtained from **ores** is only used once. When the metal article is no longer any use it is thrown away. The continual use of nonrenewable resources results in a resource scarcity.

respiration The chemical reactions by which organisms release **energy** from food such as **glucose**. Respiration may occur in the presence or in the absence of **oxygen**.

(a) *Aerobic respiration* occurs in the presence of oxygen within the *mitochondria* of **cells**.

glucose + oxygen → carbon dioxide + water
$C_6H_{12}O_6$ + $6O_2$ $6CO_2$ + $6H_2O$

(b) *Anaerobic respiration* occurs in the absence of oxygen within the cytoplasm of cells. It provides less energy than aerobic respiration.

$$\text{glucose} \xrightarrow{\text{muscle cells}} \text{lactic acid}$$
$$C_6H_{12}O_6 \qquad\qquad 2CH_3CHOHCOOH$$

Fermentation is a form of anaerobic respiration.

glucose → ethanol + carbon dioxide
$C_6H_{12}O_6$ $2C_2H_5OH$ + $2CO_2$

reversible reaction A reaction which can go either way depending on the reaction conditions, e.g.

$$Fe_2O_3(s) + 3H_2(g) \rightleftharpoons 2Fe(s) + 3H_2O(g)$$

Hydrogen can react with iron(III) oxide or steam can react with **iron**. In both cases an **equilibrium** will exist with all four substances present unless the products are removed. Reversible reactions are shown in equations by using symbol $\rightleftharpoons$.

rock cycle A process in which existing rocks are continually worn away producing **particles** which are reformed into new rocks.

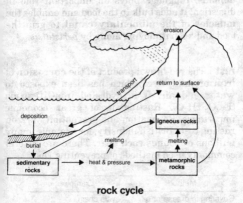

rock cycle

root The part of a flowering plant which normally grows underground in the **soil**. Its functions are:

(a) To absorb **water** and **mineral salts** from the soil.
(b) To anchor the plant in the soil.
(c) To act as a food store in some plants, such as the turnip and carrot.

roughage or **fibre** A component of the human **balanced diet**, consisting mainly of **cellulose** from plant cell walls. Although indigestible to humans, roughage plays an important role in digestion. It adds bulk to the food and enables the **muscles** of the **alimentary canal** to grip the food and keep it moving along by *peristalsis*.

rust The red-brown product of the **corrosion** of **iron** or mild **steel** which has been exposed to **water** and **air**. It is hydrated iron(III) oxide ($Fe_2O_3.xH_2O$). Rusting is of great economic importance. Renovation and prevention work on rusting costs British industry, for example, many millions of pounds each year. There are several commonly used methods of preventing rust.

Method	Example
Covering in grease or oil	cycle chain
Covering in paint	motor car body
Covering in plastic	wire mesh fencing
Electroplating	chrome car bumper
Galvanizing	coal bunker
Sacrificial protection	ship's hull

saliva Fluid secreted by the salivary glands into the mouths of many animals. Its function is to moisten and lubricate food so that it can be swallowed more easily. In some mammals, including humans, saliva contains the **enzyme** salivary amylase (sometimes called *ptyalin*) which digests **starch** into maltose.

salt This is a **compound** formed when the **hydrogen** of an **acid** is totally or partially replaced by a **metal**. When an acid reacts with a metal the result is a salt and hydrogen gas, e.g.

$$Zn(s) + 2HCl(aq) \rightarrow ZnCl_2(aq) + H_2(g)$$

When an acid reacts with a **base** the result is a salt and **water**, e.g.

$$NaOH(aq) + HNO_3(aq) \rightarrow NaNO_3(aq) + H_2O(l)$$

Salts may sometimes also be made by the direct combination of two **elements**, e.g.

$$2Na(s) + Cl_2(g) \rightarrow 2NaCl(s)$$

If only one hydrogen **atom** of a *dibasic acid* is replaced the result is an *acid salt*, e.g. sodium hydrogen carbonate $NaHCO_3$. The name of the salt is derived from the metal and the acid used.

sulphuric acid→ sulphates
nitric acid→ nitrates
hydrochloric acid→ chlorides

For example, the name of the salt formed by the reaction of copper(II) oxide and dilute sulphuric acid is copperII sulphate.

$$CuO(s) + H_2SO_4(aq) \rightarrow CuSO_4(aq) + H_2O(l)$$

secondary sexual characteristics The features which distinguish between adult male and female animals (excluding the reproductive organs). For example, the lion's mane and the antlers on a stag. In humans, secondary sexual characteristics include breast development in females and facial hair in males. The development of these features is usually controlled by **hormones**. Compare **primary sexual characteristics**.

sedimentary rocks Rocks which are formed in layers at the earth's surface. The layers may be formed:
(a) From fragments of rock produced by **weathering** and **erosion**.
(b) By chemical precipitation of dissolved substances.
(c) From the remains of plants and animals.
Sedimentary rocks are classified in terms of their composition.

Rock	Main **minerals** present
Limestone	Carbonate minerals calcite and dolomite
Sandstone	Quartz

They may also be classified in terms of their

grain size. The following rocks may have similar composition but differ in grain size.

Rock	Diameter of grains in mm
Conglomerate	more than 2
Sandstone	1/16–2
Siltstone	1/256–1/16
Mudstone	less than 1/256

See **rock cycle**.

seed This develops from an ovule after **fertilization** in flowering plants. The seeds of a plant are enclosed in a **fruit** (which develops from the **ovary**).

Within the seed, the **embryo** becomes differentiated into an embryonic **shoot** bud (plumule) and **root** (radicle) and either one or two seed leaves (cotyledons). Given the right conditions, **germination** will occur and the seed will grow into a new plant. See **fruit and seed dispersal**.

seed Section through (a) bean seed (b) maize grain.

selective breeding The breeding of animals or plants in order to enhance particular desirable features in their offspring. For example, by breeding only from the cows in a dairy herd which give the highest milk yields, the average milk yield of the whole herd might be expected to increase in time.

sensitivity The ability of plants and animals to respond to **stimuli**, such as **heat**, **light**, **sound**, etc., resulting from changes in their **environment**. Sensitivity makes organisms aware of changes in their environment, thus they can make appropriate responses to any changes which occur. Certain parts of animals, such as the **eyes**, **ears** and **skin**, are specialized in sensing particular environmental stimuli. They are called sense organs or receptors. Similarly, plant **tissues** such as *shoot tips* are receptors and are important in **tropisms**.

Stimuli from the environment cause responses

sensitivity Stimuli from the environment affect the behaviour of an organism.

to be initiated in specialized structures called *effectors*. The **muscles** in our bodies are examples of effectors. The responses which an organism makes constitute its *behaviour*. See **nervous system**.

sexual reproduction   A form of reproduction which involves the fusing of two sex cells (**gametes**), one from a male parent and the other from a female parent, to form a zygote. The fusing process is called **fertilization**. The gametes are haploid; however, the resulting zygote has a diploid number of **chromosomes**. After fertilization the zygote divides repeatedly, ultimately resulting in a new organism.

Unlike **asexual reproduction**, the offspring of sexual reproduction are genetically unique (with the exception of identical twins) because they have obtained half of their chromosomes from their male parent and half from their female parent. Thus each fertilization produces a new combination of chromosomes unique to the new organism formed.

shadow   A dark shape cast on a surface by an object through which light, a form of **radiation**, cannot pass, as radiation travels in a straight line through a given medium. If the source of radiation is small, and the object large, a sharp shadow is formed.

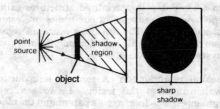

shadow A sharp shadow.

However, if the source is larger than the object the shadow formed is not sharp and shows two distinct regions. The *umbra*, or full shadow, at

shadow Shadow showing the umbra and penumbra.

the centre, surrounded by the *penumbra*, or partial shadow. No radiation reaches the umbra but some reaches the penumbra. See second diagram above.

See also **eclipse**.

shoot   The part of a plant which is above the **soil**. This is often composed of the **stem**, **leaves**, buds and **flowers**.

short circuit   A path of low **resistance** between two points in a **circuit**. The large flow of **charge** which results from a short circuit draws a heavy **current** from the source. The **heat** produced by this current should be enough to melt the **fuse** and break the circuit before any damage is done to the wiring of the circuit or the load.

SI units   The units in which scientific measurements are usually taken (Système International d'Unités). There are seven base units including:

length	metre	m
mass	kilogram	kg
time	second	s

Other units are derived from these base units, e.g.

volume	cubic metres	m^3
density	kilograms per cubic metre	kg/m^3
acceleration	metres per second per second	m/s^2

Some derived units are rather complicated and have been given special names, e.g. for **pressure**; the derived unit is the kilogram metre per second per second per square metre $(kgm/s^2)/m^2$. This is more normally called the **pascal** (Pa).

The size of a unit can be altered by using a series of prefixes.

Prefix	Symbol	Meaning
micro	μ	$\times 10^{-6}$ ($\times 1/1\,000\,000$)
milli	m	$\times 10^{-3}$ ($\times 1/1000$)
kilo	k	$\times 10^{3}$ ($\times 1000$)
mega	M	$\times 10^{6}$ ($\times 1\,000\,000$)

For example:

$$1 \text{ millimetre} = 10^{-3} \text{ metre}$$
$$1000 \text{ millimetres} = 1 \text{ metre}$$
$$1 \text{ kilometre} = 1000 \text{ metres}$$
$$0.001 \text{ kilometre} = 1 \text{ metre}$$

skeleton The hard framework of an animal which supports and protects the internal **organs** and gives the animal shape. It also provides a structure for **muscle** attachment and works with muscles to produce movement. In some animals the skeleton lies outside the body and in others the skeleton is contained within the body.

(a) *Exoskeleton* (or external skeleton). A skeleton lying outside the body of some invertebrates. Common examples are the tough *cuticle* of insects and the hard shells of crabs. Some organisms have the ability to shed and renew their exoskeletons periodically to allow **growth**. This process is called *moulting* or *ecdysis*.

skeleton   Two examples of exoskeletons.

(b) *Endoskeleton* (or internal skeleton). A skeleton lying within an animal's body. For example, the bony skeleton of vertebrates such as humans. (See diagram on page 248.) Endoskeletons get bigger as part of the growth process of an animal.

skin   A protective layer of **cells**, connective tissue and associated structures that covers most of the body of vertebrates.

   The skin of mammals can be divided into two main layers.
(a) The outer layer is the *epidermis*. It consists of:
   (i) The *cornified layer*. Dead cells which form a tough protective outer coat.
   (ii) The *granular layer*. Living cells which eventually die and form the cornified layer.
   (iii) The *Malpigian layer*. Cells which are actively dividing to produce new epidermis.
(b) The inner layer is called the *dermis*. It is a thicker layer than the epidermis and contains

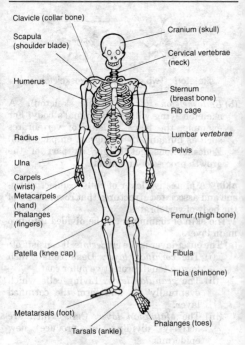

Clavicle (collar bone)

Cranium (skull)

Scapula (shoulder blade)

Cervical vertebrae (neck)

Humerus

Sternum (breast bone)

Rib cage

Radius

Lumbar *vertebrae*

Pelvis

Ulna

Carpels (wrist)

Metacarpels (hand)

Phalanges (fingers)

Femur (thigh bone)

Patella (knee cap)

Fibula

Tibia (shinbone)

Metatarsals (foot)

Phalanges (toes)

Tarsals (ankle)

skeleton The main features of the human endoskeleton.

blood capillaries, hair follicles, sweat glands, receptor cells sensitive to touch, **heat**, cold, pain and **pressure**.

Beneath the dermis there is a layer of **fat** storage cells. These cells act as a food store for the body and also provide heat **insulation**.

The functions of the mammalian skin are:

(a) Protects against injury and the entry of microorganisms which may be harmful to the body.

(b) Reduces water loss by **evaporation**.

(c) Acts as a receptor for certain environmental **stimuli**.

(d) In *homiothermic animals* (animals whose body temperatures remain fairly constant despite environmental conditions) it is important in body **temperature regulation**.

skin Section through mammalian skin.

smell The ability of animals to detect odours.

In humans the nose is the **organ** of smell. The receptor cells involved are in the nasal cavity. They are sensitive to chemical **stimuli**. See **sensitivity**.

sodium   A soft grey metallic **element** from **group** I of the **periodic table**. The **metal** is easily cut with a knife to reveal a silvery surface which rapidly tarnishes on exposure to **air**. Sodium reacts vigorously with cold **water**.

$$2Na(s) + 2H_2O(l) \rightarrow 2NaOH(aq) + H_2(g)$$

sodium   water   sodium   hydrogen
                             hydroxide

Sodium is stored under oil because of its reactivity to air and water.

Sodium metal is obtained by the **electrolysis** of molten sodium chloride. It is used as a coolant in fast-breeder nuclear reactors and in the manufacture of the petrol additive tetraethyl lead (see **lead**).

Sodium **ions** (Na^+) are an important constituent of the fluids in animal **tissues**. One way in which humans obtain sufficient sodium is to add salt (sodium chloride) to food either during cooking or when eating; however, excessive amounts of sodium cause damage to the body. There are several compounds of sodium which figure prominently in our everyday lives.

(a) *Sodium carbonate* (Na_2CO_3). This compound

is made in the Solvay process. It is important in the manufacture of glass. Unlike most carbonates, sodium carbonate does not decompose when heated. Its aqueous solution is alkaline. It may be used to remove permanent hardness from water (see **hardness of water**).

(b) *Sodium chloride* (NaCl). Known as common salt, and obtained from rock salt. As well as its use for flavouring and preserving foods, it is used in the production of sodium metal and sodium hydroxide.

(c) *Sodium hydrogencarbonate* ($NaHCO_3$). Commonly called baking powder. It is decomposed either by heat or by the action of **acids**.

$$2NaHCO_3(s) \xrightarrow{\text{heat}} Na_2CO_3(s) + CO_2(g) + H_2O$$

sodium   sodium   carbon   water
hydrogen-   carbonate
carbonate

$$NaHCO_3(s) + HCl(aq) \rightarrow NaCl(aq) + H_2O(l) + CO_2(g)$$

sodium   **hydrochloric**   sodium   water   **carbon**
hydrogen-   **acid**   chloride   **dioxide**
carbonate

Sodium hydrogencarbonate is also used in fire extinguishers and anti-indigestion powders.

(d) *Sodium hydroxide* (NaOH). This is made by the electrolysis of brine. It is a caustic **alkali** (it will corrode and burn organic material such as flesh) and solutions have **pH** > 10. It has many uses in industry, e.g. in the manufacture of soap and paper.

(e) *Sodium nitrate* ($NaNO_3$). This is used as a **fertilizer** and in the preservation of meat.

(f) *Sodium sulphate* (Na_2SO_4). The hydrated form of this salt (.$10H_2O$) is commonly known as Glauber's Salt. The sulphate is used in the manufacture of paper.

(g) *Sodium thiosulphate* ($Na_2S_2O_3$). This compound is used in the photographic process. It is used to *fix* the negative and is often called *hypo*. It reacts with unreacted silver bromide, thus ensuring that no further reaction with light occurs.

soil   The uppermost layer of the earth's crust. A typical sample of soil contains the following components.

(a) Inorganic **particles** — the result of **weathering** of rocks.

(b) **Water**.

(c) **Humus** — organic material.

(d) **Air**.

(e) **Mineral salts**.

(f) Microorganisms.

(g) Other larger organisms such as earthworms.

Soil is important for several reasons.

(a) It provides a habitat for a wide range of organisms.

(b) It provides plants with a medium for growth and supplies them with water and mineral salts.

(c) The decomposition of dead organisms in soil releases minerals which can be reused by other living organisms.

soil The composition of soil.

Soil is often classified into three distinct types.

(a) *Sandy (light) soil*. This contains a high proportion of larger inorganic particles and hence large air spaces between them. Thus sandy soils are well aerated and have good drainage. Unfortunately good drainage also tends to allow leaching (washing out) of mineral salts.

(b) *Clay (heavy) soil*. This has a high proportion of small particles and hence small air spaces. It retains mineral salts and water but is poorly aerated and may easily become waterlogged.

(c) *Loam soil*. This consists of a balance of particle types and a good humus content. The soil is well aerated and drains well whilst retaining water and mineral salts. Loam is the most fertile soil.

Sandy soil

water

large air spaces

large particles

water

Clay soil

small particles and small air spaces

(a)

(b)

soil   (a) Sandy soil. (b) Clay soil.

solar cell A device which converts **energy** from the **sun** into electrical energy by a photovoltaic process.

solar system This consists of the **sun**, nine **planets**, some with natural satellites or moons, and many asteroids, meteors and comets. The earth is the third nearest planet to the sun. See Appendix J.

solid A substance whose **atoms** or **molecules** are fixed in positions and do not have the freedom of movement found in a **liquid** or a **gas**. Atoms and molecules are held in a lattice by **bonds**. It is only when these bonds are broken that the atoms and molecules are able to move and the solid *melts*.

solubility The extent to which a solute dissolves in a solvent. In general the solubility of a particular solute increases as the **temperature** of the solvent increases.

In a polar solvent, an **ionic compound** will have a higher solubility than a **covalent compound**. For example, in **water**, sodium chloride is much more soluble than **methane**. Solubility is usually measured in grams of solute per 100 g of solvent at a stated temperature. However other units such as mole/dm^3 and mole/100 g are also used.

sound A form of **radiation** in which **energy** is transferred by means of **pressure waves** in matter, hence sound waves cannot travel through a **vacuum**. A vibrating source pushes particles of matter closer together; as they move apart they move further away from each other than their original positions. This results in alternating high and low pressure regions in the matter. A plot of pressure in the medium at different points at a given time produces a sine wave. A similar pattern is produced by plotting the pressure at a point as time passes.

Sound is thus a wave and shows all wave properties; **absorption**, **reflection**, **refraction**,

diffraction and *interference*. However sound is a *longitudinal* wave and cannot be polarized.

Like other waves, pressure waves have a **frequency spectrum**. The approximate range of sound which can be detected by the human ear is 20–20 000 Hz. Radiation from the region below 20 Hz is known as *infrasound* and from the region above 20 000 Hz is known as *ultrasound* (see **ultrasonics**). See **speed of sound**.

species   A unit used in the **classification** of living organisms. It describes any group of organisms which share the same general physical characteristics and can mate and produce fertile offspring. For example dogs, despite a wide variation in shape and size, are all of the same species.

spectrum   A type of graph which shows how different types of **radiation** relate to wavelength (and **energy**). For example, **electromagnetic**

spectrum   Typical wavelengths.

waves appear on the electromagnetic spectrum. Visible **light** is a part of this spectrum. See **colour**.

speed (c) The rate of change of distance. The unit of distance is the metre per second, m/s. Speed is a scalar measure since the direction of movement is not important. This makes it different from **velocity** which is a *vector* quantity.

speed of light or **velocity of light** The speed of light in empty space, 300 000 000 m/s. In space all **electromagnetic waves** travel at this speed. In matter they move more slowly at speeds which depend on the nature of the substance and the wavelength. See **refraction**.

speed of sound The speed of sound travelling through matter depends on the **elasticity** of the medium and its **density**. The density and elasticity of **solids** and **liquids** are far higher than those of **gases**, hence the speed of sound is lowest in gases.

The speed of sound in a particular substance increases with **temperature**. Objects moving through air at a speed greater than sound have *supersonic* speeds and shock waves form around them. These cause Concorde's *sonic boom* and the crack of a long whip.

sperm or **spermatozoon** A microscopic mal
gamete formed in animal **testes**. A sperm usu
ally has a *flagellum* and is able to move. Sperm
are released from the male in order to fertiliz
the female gamete. See **fertilization**.

spinal cord The part of the central **nervou
system** of a vertebrate which is enclosed withi
and protected by the backbone. It is a cylindrica
mass of *nerve cells* which connects the **brain** t
the other parts of the body via the spinal nerves
There are three distinct regions in the spina
cord.
(a) An inner layer of grey matter which consist
    of nerve cell bodies.
(b) An outer layer of white matter which consist
    of nerve fibres running the length of the cord
(c) A fluid-filled central canal.

   The spinal cord conducts *nerve impulses* to an

spinal cord A section through the spinal
cord.

om the brain and is also involved in **reflex ctions**.

pleen An **organ** in the abdomen. In most ertebrates it is found near the **stomach**. It has everal important functions:

) It produces **white blood cells**.

) It destroys worn out **red blood cells**.

) It filters foreign bodies from the **blood**.

pore A (usually) microscopic reproductive nit consisting of one or several **cells** which have ecome detached from the parent organism and ill ultimately become a new individual. Spores re involved in both **asexual** and **sexual** eproduction (as **gametes**). They are produced y certain plants, **fungi**, **bacteria** and protozoa. ome spores form a resistant resting stage dur- g a life cycle while others allow a rapid col- ization of new **habitats**.

sporangium *spores* — *spores being released*

hypha — } *mycelium*

spore Spore release in the bread mould *Mucor*.

amen The male part of the **flower**. Each amen consists of a stalk (filament) and at the

end of each filament there is an anther. With
the anthers there are **pollen** grains containi
the male **gametes**. See **fertilization** in plants.

filament

pollen
sac
of anther

pollen grai

pollen
sac

stamen Stamen, with anther cut open.

star A heavenly body, like the **sun**, which pr
uces its own **light**. The brightness of a star
indicated by its *magnitude*: the smaller t
magnitude, the brighter the star. The source
the **energy** emitted by stars is nuclear **fusion**.

starch A *polysaccharide* **carbohydrate** whi
consists of chains of **glucose** units. Starch
important as an **energy** store in plants, and
synthesized by plants during **photosynthesis**.
is readily converted into glucose by *amyla*
enzymes.

states of matter Substances can exist in thr
states of matter; **solid**, **liquid** and **gas**. The sta
in which a substance exists depends upon
temperature and the **pressure** exerted on
Not all substances exist in all states. The init
letters (s) = solid, (l) = liquid, (g) = gas, (a

(aq) = aqueous solution) are sometimes used in chemical **equations** to show the states of the reactants and products, e.g.

$$2Na(s) + 2H_2O(l) \rightarrow 2NaOH(aq) + H_2(g)$$

static electricity Stationary electric charges, as opposed to moving ones, i.e. current. Static often appears on an insulator when it is rubbed and charge may last for a long time. The discharge of static which has built up on a gramophone record can be heard as a 'crackle'. The discharge of static is a potential hazard in areas such as mines, factories and aircraft fuelling systems. A spark in the presence of inflammable material in the air may result in an explosion.

steel Steels are **alloys** which contain **iron** as the main constituent. Other elements present will determine the properties of the steel. The two best known types of steel are *mild steel* and *stainless steel*.

(a) Mild steel contains iron with small amounts of **carbon**. It is used for car bodies and household goods such as freezers and cookers. It is cheap to make, but it **rusts** easily in the presence of moisture and oxygen and so it must be protected. Common methods of protection are painting, greasing, enamelling, galvanizing and coating in plastic.

(b) Stainless steel contains iron, carbon, chromium and nickel. Common uses of stainless steel are cutlery, surgical instruments and sink tops. It is not corroded by oxygen, however its use is limited because it is much more expensive to produce than mild steel.

The iron made in a **blast furnace** contains impurities which make it brittle, e.g. carbon (more than is needed for mild steel). This iron is made into steel by blowing oxygen through the molten iron and thus oxidizing the impurities which are given off as **gases**. When this is done other **elements** are added to the melt to produce the steel required.

stem   The part of a flowering plant which bears the buds, **leaves** and **flowers**. The functions of the stem are:

(a) To transport **water**, **mineral salts** and **carbohydrate**.

(b) To raise the leaves above the soil so they get the maximum amount of **air** and **light**.

(c) To raise flowers, thus aiding the process of **pollination**.

(d) In green stems, **photosynthesis**.

stimulus   Any change in for example **temperature** or **pressure** in the **environment** of an organism which may produce a response in the organism. See **sensitivity**.

Young stem
transverse section

Young stem
longitudinal section

cortex
xylem
epidermis
cambium
phloem

phloem
xylem

(a)

Older stem
transverse section

Older stem
longitudinal section

xylem
(wood)
bark
phloem

phloem
xylem
(wood)

(b)

stem The structure of (a) younger and (b) older dicotyledon stems.

stomach A muscular sac in the anterior region of the **alimentary canal**. In vertebrates food passes into the stomach from the mouth via the oesophagus.

In the stomach, food is mechanically churned by the peristaltic action of the muscular walls and the **digestion** of **protein** is started. In herbivores the stomach has several chambers, for cellulose digestion.

The amount of time which food spends in the stomach depends on its nature. From the stomach it passes into the small intestine through a ring of muscle called the *pyloric sphincter*.

structural formula The formula of a substance which shows the **bonds** between its **atoms** and their positions relative to each other.

ethane
C_2H_6

ethanol
C_2H_5OH

molecular formula   structural formula

> **structural formula** The structural formula gives more information than the **molecular formula**.

sucrose A **carbohydrate** belonging to the group of **sugars** called *disaccharides*. Sucrose is the white crystalline substance which we use at home and commonly call sugar. It is obtained from sugar beet or sugar cane.

sugar A common name for a series of sweet **compounds** which are either monosaccharides or disaccharides. For example:
(a) monosaccharides – **glucose**, fructose, ribose.
(b) disaccharides – maltose, **sucrose**.
See **carbohydrate**.

sulphur (S₈) A yellow nonmetallic **element** which may exist in two forms or *allotropes*. *Rhombic sulphur* is the stable form below 96 °C and *monoclinic sulphur* is stable above that **temperature**.

Sulphur belongs to **group** VI of the **periodic table** and is reactive to both **metals** and **nonmetals**. It occurs in nature both uncombined and as metal sulphides such as galena (PbS) and pyrite (FeS). Sulphur and sulphur-containing compounds are also found in **petroleum**, **natural gas** and **coal**. Such impurities are a problem as the **combustion** of any **fuel** containing them will produce sulphur dioxide, one of the main causes of **acid rain**. In modern processes sulphur and sulphur-containing compounds are either removed from fuels before combustion, or any sulphur dioxide gas produced is removed from the exhaust gases. Sulphur is an important constituent of some drugs, such as *sulphonamides*, and is used to vulcanize rubber; however, its main use is in the manufacture of **sulphuric acid** in the contact process.

sulphuric acid (H₂SO₄) A very important chemical used in many processes. It is a colourless, oily **liquid** which is a strong **acid** and a vigorous oxidizing agent (see **oxidation**). It is made from *sulphur dioxide* in the *contact process*. Sulphuric acid reacts chemically in several ways:

(a) **As an acid.** Dilute sulphuric acid reacts with **metals**, **bases** and *carbonates* to form *sulphates*.

$$Mg(s) + H_2SO_4(aq) \rightarrow MgSO_4(aq) + H_2(g)$$
$$CuO(s) + H_2SO_4(aq) \rightarrow CuSO_4(aq) + H_2O(l)$$
$$ZnCO_3(s) + H_2SO_4(aq) \rightarrow ZnSO_4(aq) + H_2O(l) + CO_2(g)$$

sulphuric acid   The contact process.

Concentrated sulphuric acid reacts with chlorides and nitrates to form hydrogen chloride and nitric acid respectively.

$$H_2SO_4(l) + NaCl \rightarrow NaHSO_4(s) + HCl(g)$$
$$H_2SO_4(l) + NaNO_3 \rightarrow NaHSO_4(s) + HNO_3(g)$$

(b) **As a dehydrating agent.** Concentrated sulphuric acid is sometimes used to dry **gases**. It can also be used to remove the **atoms** which make **water** from substances.

(c) As an *oxidizing agent*. Although **copper** cannot directly replace **hydrogen** from acids, the metal is oxidized by concentrated sulphuric acid.

$$Cu(s) + 2H_2SO_4(l) \rightarrow CuSO_4(s) + SO_2(g) + 2H_2O(l)$$

                 anhydrous
                 copper(II)
                 sulphate

The reaction between concentrated sulphuric acid and water is a very **exothermic reaction**. When diluting concentrated sulphuric acid, it is important always to add the acid to the water (by stirring) and NOT the other way around.

sun The **star** at the centre of the **solar system**. The sun is the source of most of the **energy** available on **earth** either directly, as **light** and **heat**, or indirectly, as the source of energy for plant **growth**. The earth's axis is permanently tilted at an angle of 66.5° to the plane of its orbit. The tilting of the axis is responsible for the following:

(a) The changes in the altitude of the midday sun throughout the year. The sun is highest at midday on June 21st (*summer solstice*) and lowest at midday on December 22nd (*winter solstice*).

(b) The variation in length of the days (and nights) throughout the year. The longest day is June 21st and the shortest December 22nd.

(c) The four seasons.

In the summer in Britain the weather is generally warmer. This is the result of the sun being higher in the sky (the sun's rays are more intense) and the longer day length. In the winter the weather is generally colder. The sun's rays are less intense and day length is shorter.

sun The tilting of the earth's axis is responsible for the difference in the seasons.

taste The ability of animals to detect flavours. In humans the receptor cells for taste are called taste buds. They are sensitive to certain chemical **stimuli**. They are restricted to the mouth, particularly on the tongue. There are four types of taste bud sensitive to sweet, sour, salt and bitter. Taste and **smell** often work together to identify different foods. See **sensitivity**.

taste A taste map of the tongue.

tectonic theory This theory considers the crust of the **earth** to be made of huge rigid blocks called plates. There are seven major plates together with several minor ones.

The plates are thought to slide on molten **magma**. Plates meet along *plate boundaries* and the areas near to the plate boundaries are called *plate margins*. The process of forming new geological structures, as a result of the movement of plates, is called *plate tectonics*. See **earthquake**, **volcano**.

teeth Structures within the mouths of vertebrates which are used for biting, tearing and crushing food before it is swallowed.

Enamel. This covers the exposed surface of the tooth (the crown). It contains calcium phosphate and is the hardest substance in a vertebrate's body. It is well suited to biting food without itself being damaged.

Dentine. This substance is similar to **bone** and forms the inner part of the tooth.

Pulp. The soft **tissue** in the centre of the tooth. It contains the **blood capillaries**, which supply food and **oxygen**, and the nerve fibres which register pain if the tooth is damaged.

Root. The part of the tooth within the gum and embedded in the jawbone. The outer surface of the root is covered in a substance called cement. A series of fibres hold the tooth in place. One end of them is embedded in the cement and the other in the jawbone.

Most human beings are *omnivores*. The adult human jaw contains four types of teeth.

Incisors. Chisel-shaped teeth at the front of the mouth used for biting off pieces of food.

Canines. Pointed teeth at each side of the incisors. They are used for ripping off pieces of food. In wild animals which are carnivores, such as lions and tigers, these teeth are often very large and also used for killing prey. In herbivores these teeth are often small or missing completely.

teeth Tooth structure.

Premolars. Grinding teeth found between the canines and the molars.

Molars. Together with premolars these teeth are often called *cheek teeth* because of the position they occupy at the back of the mouth. They are broad-crowned teeth which crush and grind food before it is swallowed. They are found in both herbivores and omnivores but in carnivores they are replaced by *carnassial* teeth.

See **dental formula**.

teeth The arrangement of teeth in an adult human jaw (bottom and top jaws are the same).

telescope An optical instrument which produces enlarged images of distant objects. There are several different types of telescope in common use.

(a) A Galilean telescope (as in opera glasses) combines a converging and a diverging **lens**.

(b) A standard refracting telescope has two converging lenses. This produces more magnification than a Galilean type but the tube needs to be much longer and the image produced is upside down.

(c) A reflecting telescope has a converging **mirror** in place of an object lens.

(d) A standard radio telescope has the same design as a reflecting telescope but it is designed to detect **radio** waves.

temperature (T)   The **heat** level of a substance. It relates to the mean **energy** of the **particles** of the sample. There are several temperature scales used to show the degree of temperature. In daily life we use *Celsius (centrigrade)* or *Fahrenheit*. In science the *absolute* scale is also commonly used.

Scale	Unit	Melting point of pure ice	Boiling point of pure water
Celsius	degree C, °C	0 °C	100 °C
Fahrenheit	degree F, °F	32 °F	212 °F
Absolute	kelvin, K	273 K	373 K

Temperature is measured using a **thermometer**.

temperature regulation   *Homoiothermic* animals maintain their body temperature within a narrow range despite the temperature of their **environment**. For example, the temperature of a healthy human being is always around 37 °C.

This is essential so that the normal reactions of **metabolism** can take place. Here are some ways in which birds and mammals regulate their temperature.

(a) Fat under the skin (subcutaneous) acts as an insulator.

(b) Hair in mammals and feathers in birds trap **air** which is a good insulator.

(c) In mammals the **evaporation** of sweat from the surface of the **skin** has a cooling effect.

(d) Blood vessels near the surface of the skin constrict in response to cold. This diverts blood away from the skin surface so less heat is lost (*vasoconstriction*).

(e) Blood vessels near the surface of the skin dilate in response to heat. This brings blood up to the skin surface so more heat is lost to the atmosphere (*vasodilation*).

testis The **sperm**-producing reproductive **organ** of male animals. Male vertebrates such as men have a pair of testes which, in addition to sperms, also produce **hormones**. See **fertilization** in humans.

thermionic emission The emission of a stream of **electrons** from a heated *filament*. The electrons are attracted to the oppositely charged *anode* and accelerated towards it. Most electrons pass through the anode and travel on towards the

thermionic emission In this apparatus electrons are emitted by the hot cathode.

fluorescent screen. Those which strike the Maltese cross are absorbed by it, casting a shadow of the cross on the screen. Streams of electrons moving at high speed are called *cathode rays*. They are the basis of the *cathode ray oscilloscope*.

thermometer A device used to measure **temperature** or 'hotness'. This relates to the mean **energy** of the **particles** of the sample. Thermometers work by measuring something which varies with temperature, e.g.:
(a) A column of **liquid** in a glass tube; as the liquid gets hotter it expands and the level rises up the tube.
(b) The **voltage** between two **metals**.
  Other properties, such as the **pressure** of a **gas**, the **resistance** of a wire, or the colour of a hot surface, may also be used. In each case the

device is used at certain known temperatures (often the **boiling** and **freezing points** of **water**) and is then marked in degrees according to the scale used.

thermoplastic A **polymer** which softens when heated and can be moulded and remoulded into new shapes. **Nylon** and *polychloroethene* are examples of thermoplastics. Compare **thermosetting plastic**.

thermosetting plastic A **polymer** which cannot be softened and reshaped by heating. The application of heat to a thermosetting plastic results in its decomposition. *Bakelite* and *formica* are examples of thermosetting plastics. Compare **thermoplastic**.

thermostat A device which is used to keep the **temperature** in a place within a particular range. Thermostats are present in a number of common household devices such as cookers, refrigerators, irons, freezers and heating boilers. Many thermostats use a **bimetallic strip**.

three-pin plug The standard method of joining a cable to a mains socket. A mains cable has three wires. These are colour-coded as shown in the table below. Each wire goes to a particular pin in the plug.

The size of the **fuse** fitted in the plug depends

on the **power** of the device to which it is connected.

Wire	Colour of plastic coating	Purpose
live	brown	carries **current**
neutral	blue	returns current
earth	green/yellow	safety

Three-pin plug

tidal barrage A wall built across a river estuary. The wall contains *turbogenerators* which transfer **kinetic energy** from the **tides** into **electricity**. There are no tidal barrages currently operating in Britain but studies have been carried out on several river estuaries (including the Mersey and Severn) with a view to building tidal barrages in the future. See **renewable energy sources**.

tide The alternating rise and fall of the sea which occurs about every twelve hours. Tides are due to the gravitational pull of the **moon** and, to a lesser extent, the gravitational pull of the **sun**.

tide Spring tides.

Spring tides occur when the moon, earth and sun are in a straight line. The combined pull of the moon and sun result in very high tides and equally low tides. The difference in the level of the sea at high tide and low tide is very large.

tide Neap tides.

Neap tides occur when the pull of the sun is at right angles to that of the moon. The difference in the level of the sea at high tide and low tide is quite small.

tissue In **multicellular** organisms tissue is a group of similar **cells** which are specialized to carry out a specific function within the organism. For example, **muscle** in animals and xylem in plants. The human body contains many different types of tissue.

transformer A device normally used to transfer electrical **energy** with a change in **voltage**.

An **alternating current** input to the primary coil causes an alternating magnetic field in the core of the transformer. In turn, this changing field induces an alternating current at the secondary (output) coil. The ratio of the output voltage to the input voltage equals the ratio of the number of turns of wire in the output and input coils, i.e.:

$$\frac{V_2}{V_1} = \frac{N_2}{N_1}$$

For a *step down* transformer, $V_2 < V_1$ hence $N_2 < N_1$, and for a *step up* transformer the reverse applies $V_2 > V_1$ hence $N_2 > N_1$. The electrical power in the coil of a transformer is calculated by multiplying the current passing through the coil by the voltage across it. The **efficiency** of a transformer is often measured as the ratio of useful output power to total input power.

$$\text{efficiency} = \frac{\text{useful output power}}{\text{total input power}}$$

No energy transfer device has an efficiency of 100%; however, many transformers are very close to this. See **electromagnetic induction**.

transformer

transistor A semiconductor device whose output **current** depends on signals to the base. Its main uses are in amplifiers and oscillators.

transpiration The **evaporation** of water vapour from plant leaves via tiny pores called *stomata*. The rate at which transpiration occurs depends on several environmental factors.
(a) **Temperature** — increased temperature increases the rate at which water evaporates and thus increases transpiration.
(b) Humidity (water content of air) — increased

humidity causes the atmosphere to become saturated with water vapour, thus reducing transpiration.

(c) Wind — increased air movements increase the rate at which water evaporates by preventing the atmosphere immediately around the stomata from becoming saturated; thus it increases the rate of transpiration.

It follows from the above that the transpiration rate will be greatest in warm, dry, windy conditions. If the rate of water loss by transpiration exceeds the rate of water uptake through the **roots** the plant may begin to wilt.

tropisms In plant **growth**, movement in response to a **stimulus** such as **light**. These movements are related to the direction of the stimulus, the plant organ growing either towards or away from it. Tropisms are named by adding a prefix which refers to the stimulus involved:

(a) *Geotropism* — a response to gravity.

(b) *Phototropism* — a response to light.

(c) *Chemotropism* — a response to chemicals.

(d) *Hydrotropism* — a response to water.

Tropisms can be either positive or negative depending on whether the response is in the same direction or the opposite direction to the stimulus. They are important because they allow plants to grow in such a way that they can get the maximum benefit from their **environment** in terms of water, light, etc.

Tropisms are caused by a plant **hormone** or *auxin* which accelerates growth by stimulating cell division and elongation. Uneven distribution of auxins causes uneven growth which eventually leads to bending.

ultrasound Sound waves of higher frequency than can be detected by the human ear (about 20 kHz). Some other animals are able to hear some of the ultrasonic range. For example, the *sonar* system of bats typically works at 50 kHz or higher. Ultrasound of megahertz frequencies has many uses in modern life. For example, detecting explosive mines at sea, checking on babies in the womb (typical value 2.25 MHz), and cleaning engine parts.

ultraviolet A region in the **spectrum** of **electromagnetic waves**. The approximate wavelength range is 10^{-10}–10^{-7} m and the approximate **frequency** range is 10^{15}–10^{18} Hz. Ultraviolet **radiation** is produced by white-hot objects and certain **gas** discharges. It affects photographic film and causes fluorescence and photo-electric effects. Human **skin** makes **vitamin** D with this radiation and light skins are tanned by it. However, over-exposure is harmful to both the **eyes** and skin. The **ozone layer** limits the amount of ultraviolet radiation which reaches the earth's surface.

unicellular (of an organism) Consisting of only one **cell**. Unicellular organisms include protozoans, **bacteria** and some algae. Compare **multicellular**.

uranium This **element** is a **metal** which has 92 **protons**. Its **atoms** are the most massive of all natural elements. Uranium has three **isotopes**; uranium-234, uranium-235 and uranium-238. All three are radioactive, being sources of **alpha particles**.

The **nuclei** of uranium-235 atoms can undergo nuclear **fission** when they absorb **neutrons**. The process of nuclear fission itself produces more neutrons. Under certain conditions, a **chain reaction** may take place. This is the basis of **nuclear power** and the atomic bomb.

urea The main nitrogenous excretory product of mammals. Urea is made in the **liver** as a product of the *deamination* of excess **amino acids**. It travels from the liver to the **kidney** via the bloodstream and is excreted in the **urine**.

$$H_2N-\underset{\underset{O}{\|}}{C}-NH_2 \text{ urea}$$

urine An aqueous solution of **urea** and salts produced by the **kidneys** of mammals. It is stored in the bladder before being discharged via the urethra.

uterus or **womb** A muscular cavity found in most female mammals. The uterus contains the **embryo** during its development. It receives **ova** from the oviduct and connects to the exterior of the body via the vagina. See **fertilization** in humans, **menstrual cycle**, **pregnancy**.

vaccine A mixture containing dead or inactivated microorganisms normally responsible for a disease. It is given to stimulate (see **stimulus**) an *immune response* in a person from which he or she gains immunity to the disease. Vaccines are not quick-acting but rely on the gradual build up of **antibodies** in the person's **blood**. See **immunization**.

vacuum A space from which the **air** has been removed, thus containing very few **particles** of matter. A cubic metre of air at standard pressure contains around 10^{25} particles; a good vacuum on **earth** contains about 10^{14}. Between the earth and the **moon** the value is far lower, and between galaxies there may be a true vacuum (containing no particles). Nevertheless the vacuum of outer space contains **energy** in forms other than matter such as **force** fields, **radiation** and very low **mass** particles called neutrinos.

valency The number of **bonds** which an **atom** forms with other atoms. More precisely, the valency of an **element** is the number of **electrons** that it needs to form a **compound** or radical. The electrons may be lost, gained or shared with another atom.

Some elements always have the same valency. **Sodium** always has a valency of 1. It gives one electron away when it forms the sodium **ion** Na^+ in compounds like sodium chloride $NaCl$. **Oxygen** always has a valency of 2. It accepts two electrons when it forms the oxide ion O^{2-} or it forms **covalent compounds** such as CO_2 and SO_2. *Transition elements* have more than one valency, e.g. cobalt = 2 or 3; **copper** = 1 or 2; **iron** = 2 or 3. The table opposite shows the valencies of some common elements and the ions they form.

variation The difference in characteristics between two members of the same **species**. There are two main types of variation.

(a) *Discrete variation*. In this type of variation only particular values within a given range are possible. For example, a person's **blood** may belong to group A, B, AB or O but not somewhere between two groups, i.e. there are no possible intermediate forms. Discrete data does not show a *normal distribution*.

(b) *Continuous variation*. In this type of variation the variable may take any value within a par-

Positive values					
+1		+2		+3	
Lithium	Li$^+$	Calcium	Ca^{2+}	Aluminium	Al^{3+}
Sodium	Na$^+$	Magnesium	Mg^{2+}	Iron(III)	Fe^{3+}
Potassium	K$^+$	Zinc	Zn^{2+}		
Silver	Ag$^+$	Iron(II)	Fe^{2+}		
Ammonium	NH$_4^+$	Lead	Pb^{2+}		
Hydrogen	H$^+$	Copper(II)	Cu^{2+}		

Negative values					
−1		−2		−3	
Fluoride	F$^-$	Sulphide	S^{2-}	Phosphate PO$_4^{3-}$	
Chloride	Cl$^-$	Oxide	O^{2-}		
Bromide	Br$^-$	Carbonate	CO$_3^{2-}$		
Iodide	I$^-$	Sulphate	SO$_4^{2-}$		
Hydroxide	OH$^-$				
Nitrate	NO$_3$				

valency

ticular range. For example, if a person is between 1.90 and 1.91 m tall they may be 1.900, 1.901, 1.902 m etc. The only limitation is the accuracy with which we measure the height. Another example in humans is **mass**. Continuous variation throughout a population shows a normal distribution about an average value called the mean. (We often represent continuous data as if it were dis-

variation A continuous variation, showing the mean.

crete data by placing it in groups.)

Variation within a **species** results from either inherited or environmental factors or a combination of both. For example, a human being inherits **genes** influencing height but is also subject to environmental factors such as nutrition. Inherited variations are considered to be the basis of **evolution** by **natural selection**.

vegetative reproduction or **propagation** Asexual reproduction in plants by an out-

Form of outgrowth	Example of plant
bulb	daffodil, onion
corm	crocus, gladiolus
rhizome	iris
stolon	strawberry
tuber	potato, dahlia

growth of some kind from the parent plant. The outgrowth may occur in several different ways. The table shows some examples.

vein A **blood** vessel which transports blood from the **tissue** of the body to the **heart**. In mammals, veins carry deoxygenated blood, with the exception of the pulmonary vein which carries oxygenated blood from the **lungs** to the heart. Veins are formed from groups of smaller blood vessels called *venules* which carry blood from **capillaries**. The blood pressure in veins is less than in **arteries**, and this accounts for the differences in their structures. Veins have much thinner walls than arteries and have valves to prevent blood flowing away from the heart.

The largest veins in humans are the *superior vena cava*, which carries blood from the head, neck and upper arms to the heart, and the *inferior vena cava* which carries blood from the rest of the body to the heart.

vein (a) Section through a vein. (b) Valve operation in veins.

velocity (v)   An object's displacement in unit time. The unit used is the metre per second, m/s. Velocity is a *vector* (compare **speed**). To find velocity we divide the displacement, *s*, by the time taken, *t*; $v = s/t$. The slope at any point on a graph of displacement against time gives the velocity at that instant.

vertebral column or **backbone**   A series of interlocking bones (called *vertebrae*) and/or *cartilages* which runs along the back from the skull to the tail in vertebrates. It is the principal longitudinal supporting structure of the body. It also protects the **spinal cord** which runs down its centre. See **skeleton**.

virus   Viruses are the smallest known living organisms, having diameters between 0.025 and 0.25 microns. They are **parasites** infecting animals, plants and **bacteria**. A virus particle

| bacterium virus becomes attached to bacterium | the virus nuclear material is injected into the bacterium and causes the assembly of new virus parts | the bacterium cell wall is ruptured, releasing many new viruses |

virus   A virus infecting a bacterium.

consists of a **protein** coat surrounding a length of nucleic acid, either **DNA** or RNA.

Virus infections in humans include measles, polio and influenza.

vitamins These are organic **compounds** which are required in small amounts by living organisms. Like **enzymes**, vitamins play a vital role in chemical reactions within the body and often regulate an enzyme's action. If the human diet contains insufficient amounts of vitamins this will result in deficiency diseases.

Vitamin	Rich sources	Effects of deficiency
A	Milk, liver, butter, fresh vegetables.	Night-blindness and in children retarded growth.
B$_1$	Yeast, liver.	Beri-beri; loss of appetite and weakness.
B$_2$	Yeast, milk	Pellagra; skin infections, weakness, mental illness.
C	Citrus fruit, fresh vegetables.	Scurvy; bleeding gums, skin disorders.
D	Eggs, cod liver oil.	Rickets; abnormal bone formation.
E	Fresh green vegetables, milk.	Thought to affect reproductive ability.
K	Fresh vegetables.	Blood clotting impaired.

volcano An opening in the earth's crust through which **magma** comes to the surface of the earth as *lava*. The lava leaves the volcano through an opening called a vent. Ash and gases, including water vapour, are also given out into the air.

Volcanoes may be active, dormant or extinct. The effects of a volcanic eruption may be considerable. In AD 79, the eruption of the volcano Vesuvius buried the nearby town of Pompeii in hot ash to a depth of 3 m. When the volcano Krakatoa erupted in 1883 there was an explosion which was heard 5000 km away and around 18 km³ of material was thrown into the air. See **earthquake**.

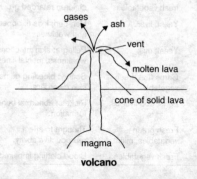

volcano

voltage or **potential difference** The electrical **pressure** which drives electric charges round a **circuit**. The unit is the volt, V. **Electricity** will only flow between two places which have a potential difference between them. One volt is the potential difference between two points which allows 1 **joule** of **energy** to be obtained when 1 *coulomb* of **charge** moves between the points.

$$\text{volts} = \text{joules/coulombs}$$

volume The amount of space taken up by an object. The **SI unit** of volume is the cubic metre, m³.

The volumes of **solids** and **liquids** are fairly constant. The volume of a **gas** depends greatly on

volume
of cuboid = a × b × c

volume
of cylinder = $\pi r^2 h$

volume
of sphere = $\frac{4}{3}\pi r^3$

volume
of cone = $\frac{1}{3}\pi r^2 h$

volume

the **temperature** and **pressure**.

water (H_2O)   An oxide of **hydrogen**,

$$2H_2(g) + O_2(g) \rightarrow 2H_2O(l)$$

water is one of the most common **compounds** on the **earth**, and is essential for all living things. It is a colourless **liquid**. Here are some of its more important properties.

Freezing point	0 °C
Boiling point	100 °C
Density	1.0 g/cm³

(the maximum density of water occurs at 4 °C)

Water is an atypical liquid, as it expands on solidification, thus ice is less dense than water and floats on it. Water pipes burst when the water in them expands into ice. Pure water does not conduct electricity; however, it can be electrolysed if small amounts of **acid** (H_2SO_4) or **alkali** (NaOH) are added. The products of this **electrolysis** are **hydrogen** and **oxygen**.

$$2H_2O(l) \rightarrow 2H_2(g) + O_2(g)$$

A substance can be tested for the presence of water by adding an **anhydrous** salt such as copper sulphate or cobalt chloride, which will change colour, since:–

$$CuSO_4(s) + 5H_2O \rightarrow CuSO_4.5H_2O(s)$$

$\quad\quad$ white $\quad\quad\quad\quad\quad\quad\quad$ blue

$$\text{CoCl}_2(s) \quad + \quad 6\text{H}_2\text{O} \quad \rightarrow \quad \text{CoCl}_2.6\text{H}_2\text{O}(s)$$

blue   pink

One way to test the purity of water is to measure its boiling point.

As well as in animals and plants, water is found in the **atmosphere**, rivers and lakes, **soil**, glaciers and the oceans. Water is continually flowing from place to place, being used and reused by plants and animals; this is represented by the **water cycle**.

The most important use of water is as a solvent. Water has polar bonds so it can dissolve ionic solids such as sodium chloride (NaCl), as well as polar solids such as **glucose** ($C_6H_{12}O_6$).

The water we drink is never pure. It always contains small amounts of **gases**, such as oxygen and **carbon dioxide**, and depending on the source of the water it may also contain dissolved solids. Some dissolved solids make the water hard. See **hardness of water**.

water cycle The continuous movement of water between the **earth** and the **atmosphere**. Water evaporates from the oceans into the atmosphere. From here it falls on the earth (in several forms, such as rain, snow, etc.) and also freezes out of the air as frost and ice. This water enters the rocks and soil and will eventually find its way back into the oceans via lakes and rivers. Plants

snow

ice cap

rainfall

transpiration

combustion
respiration

town
river

streams and
rivers

lake

clouds

evaporation

sea

and animals take water out of the ground for their own use. This water will eventually return to the atmosphere, by processes such as **transpiration**, **respiration** and sweating, or to the oceans through **excretion**. Large quantities of water are stored as ice in glaciers and in the polar ice caps.

watt The unit of **power**. This is a measure of the rate at which work is done.

(a) In mechanics:

$$\text{power (watts)} = \frac{\text{work done (\textbf{joules})}}{\text{time taken (seconds)}}$$

(b) In electricity:

$$\text{power (watts)} = \textbf{current (amperes)} \times \textbf{voltage (volts)}$$

wave A type of **radiation** (the other type consisting of particles). Most waves can be described as either *transverse* or *longitudinal*. Transverse

wave A transverse and a longitudinal wave.

waves consist of *vibrations* whose direction is across the direction of **energy** transfer. With longitudinal waves the vibration direction is the same as the direction of energy transfer.

The distance taken up by a single cycle of a wave is called the *wavelength* (λ).

The wavelength (λ), frequency (f) and speed (c) of a wave are related in the basic wave equation;

$$\text{speed} = \text{frequency} \times \text{wavelength} \; (c = f \times \lambda)$$

All waves can show **absorption**, **reflection**, **refraction**, **diffraction** and interference. See **electromagnetic waves**, **sound**, **water**.

wave Wavelength.

wave generators Devices which transfer the **kinetic energy** of the waves at sea into **electricity**. The device is sited on the shore line and the up and down movement of the water level, caused by the waves, is used to force air through a turbine which drives a **generator**.

See **renewable energy sources**.

air moves in and out through the turbine

turbine and generator

sea

water column rises and falls with wave movement

shore

sand and rock

wave generator

weather The condition of the **atmosphere**. The factors which make up the weather include rain, **temperature**, humidity, wind speed and direction (see **anemometer**, **wind vane**) and atmospheric pressure (see **barometer**).

weathering The processes (physical or chemical) by which rock is fragmented or altered. Physical processes which break rock up include:
(a) **Expansion** and contraction caused by daily **temperature** changes.
(b) The freezing and expansion of water in cracks.
Chemical weathering processes include:

(a) The dissolving of minerals in water.

(b) The reaction of minerals with **oxygen** from the air or with carbonic acid (formed when **carbon dioxide** dissolves in water).

See **erosion**.

weight (*W*) The **force** which an object exerts downwards because of gravitational attraction. Like all forces, it is measured in newtons (N). The weight of an object depends on its **mass**, m, and the strength of the gravitational field, g; $W = mg$. This gives, as a unit for g, the newton per kilogram N/kg. An object's mass is thought to be constant. The value of g depends on where the object is, hence the weight of the object also depends on where it is. On the **earth** ($g = 10$ m/s^2 or 10 N/kg), the weight of a 5 kg object is $5 \times 10 = 50$ N. On the **moon** ($g = 1.6$ m/s^2 or 1.6 N/kg), its weight would be $5 \times 1.6 = 8$ N. In a place, such as outer space, where there is very little gravitational force (i.e. $g = 0$) acting on an object its weight will be zero. See **gravity**.

white blood cell, white blood corpuscle or **leucocyte** One of the types of **blood cell** found in most vertebrates. Their function is to defend the body against microorganism infection. This is achieved in two ways.

(a) Some white blood cells produce **antibodies** which react with invading microorganisms and render them harmless.

(b) Some white blood cells engulf and digest invading microorganisms. This process is called *phagocytosis*. Compare **red blood cell**.

wind turbine A device in which **kinetic energy** from the wind is transferred into **electricity**. A huge propeller, attached to a shaft, is driven around by the wind in much the same way as the sails of a windmill. The rotating shaft is used to drive a **generator**. Wind turbines are devices which make use of **renewable energy sources**. They are often grouped together in *wind farms*.

wind vane, weather vane or **weathercock** A device which shows the direction from which the wind is blowing. It consists of a rotating arm pivoted on a vertical shaft. The arrow of the wind vane always points in the direction from which

wind blowing from the south west

wind vane

the wind blows. The rotating arm may be in the form of an animal or other shape.

X-rays A region of the **spectrum** of **electromagnetic waves**. The approximate wavelength range is 10^{-12}–10^{-10} m and the approximate **frequency** range is 10^{18}–10^{21} Hz. X-rays are produced by firing **electrons** at **metals**. It is a very penetrating **radiation** and will easily pass through flesh, but is stopped by **bone** and other dense materials. X-rays are widely used in medicine to take pictures of bones. A photographic plate is placed behind the area of the body to be investigated and the area of the body is then exposed to an X-ray source. The bones show up as light areas on the photographic plate.

yeast A general name for a group of microorganisms which are very useful to humans. Yeasts contain **enzymes** which convert **sugars** into ethanol. This process is called **fermentation**.

APPENDIX A: Abbreviations and Symbols

A list of some useful common abbreviations and symbols you may encounter in scientific literature.

A	mass number; also Ampère — unit of electric current
aq	state symbol for aqueus solution usually as (aq)
A_r	relative atomic mass
atm	atmosphere — a unit of pressure
α	alpha Greek letter
β	beta Greek letter
b.p.	boiling point
C	Celsius as in °C degree Celsius; also Coulomb — unit of electric charge (quantity of electricity)
cm^3	cubic centimetre, unit of volume
DC	direct current — the type of electricity produced from a battery
dm^3	cubic decimetre $\equiv 1$ litre, unit of volume
E	symbol for emf of a cell
e or e^-	electron
emf	electromotive force
g	gram — unit of mass; state symbol for gas usually as (g); also acceleration due to gravity
H	enthalpy (ΔH = enthalpy change)
I	electric current
J	Joule — unit of energy
k	prefix meaning 'one thousand times' i.e. $kg = 1000\ g$
K	Kelvin — unit of temperature, $1\ K \equiv 1\ °C$
l	state symbol for liquid usually as (l)
m	mass; also metre — unit of length

M	molar — unit of concentration (molarity) e.g. 2M
m^3	cubic metre — unit of volume
ml	millilitre, $\frac{1}{1000}$ of 1 litre $\equiv$ 1 cm^3
mol.	mole — unit of amount of substance
m.p.	melting point
M_r	relative molecular mass
n	neutron
N	Newton — unit of force
nm	nanometer — one thousand-millionth of a metre
NTP	Normal temperature and pressure
p	proton; also pressure
Pa	Pascal — unit of pressure
p.d.	potential difference
pH	relates to a scale of acidity, e.g. pH = 1 very strongly acidic
Q	electric charge, quantity of electricity
s	state symbol for solid usually as (s); also second — unit of time
STP	standard temperature and pressure
t	time
T	temperature
$T\frac{1}{2}$ or $t\frac{1}{2}$	half life (of radioactive isotope)
UV	ultraviolet
V	volume; also electrical potential difference (p.d.); also volt — unit of p.d.
Z	atomic number

APPENDIX B: Circuit Symbols

A list of the standard symbols and names of the main circuit elements you are likely to meet.

Conductors

———	conductor
—┼—	crossing conductors
—┿—	conductor junction
⌇	sliding contact
╱ —	simple switch
╱ —	two-way switch

Sources

—o •—	general supply to output
⊣⊢	cell (short arm is negative)
⊣⊢··⊣⊢	battery of cells
—Ⓖ—	generator
Υ	aerial

Passive elements

⊟	resistor or resistive element
⊟	fuse
}	variable resistor
⊣⊢	capacitor
⊣▮⊢	electrolytic capacitor (black arm is cathode)
⊷	inductor
▷⊢	diode (allows current to the right)
●—	signal lamp
⊝	filament lamp
⏚	earth

Electromagnet elements

—Ⓐ—	ammeter
—Ⓥ—	voltmeter
◁	speaker

microphone

 motor

transformer

Vacuum devices

 diode

cathode ray tube

Semiconductor devices

 pn junction (diode)

 light-emitting diode

photo-diode

 pnp transistor

 npn transistor

light sensitive pn diode

Sub-circuits

 gate

 amplifier

 inverter or NOT gate

 AND gate

OR gate

XOR gate

NAND gate

NOR gate

NXOR gate

APPENDIX C: Characteristics of living things

For an organism to be considered as 'living' it must demonstrate *all* of the following features:

Movement	The ability to change position either of all, or, of part of the body.
Excretion	The ability to remove from the body waste materials produced by the organism
Respiration	The ability to release energy by

	the breakdown of complex chemicals.
Reproduction	The ability to produce offspring.
Irritability	The ability to sense and respond to changes in the environment.
Nutrition	The ability to take in or manufacture food that can be used when required as a source of energy or as building materials.
Growth	The ability to increase in size and complexity through the production of new cell material.

APPENDIX D: The Differences between Plants and Animals

Plants	*Animals*
Cell surrounded by cellulose cell wall	No cellulose cell wall
Large vacuoles in cells filled with cell sap	Vacuoles when present only small
Large cells with definite shape	Small irregularly shaped cells

Only restricted movement possible	Free movement possible
Response to stimulus slow	Rapid response to stimulus
Cells contain chloroplasts (chlorophyll)	No chloroplasts (chlorophyll)
Photosynthese	Must obtain food from external sources

These characteristic differences should only be regarded as guidelines. Attempts to classify certain organisms within these terms of reference will be difficult and has provided scientists with great problems, for example, bacteria, fungi, viruses.

APPENDIX E: The Major Groups of Living Organisms

THE ANIMAL KINGDOM (major phyla)

(a) **INVERTEBRATES** Animals without a **vertebral column** (backbone)

Phylum Protozoa Microscopic **unicellular** animals.

Phylum Porifera Porous animals often occurring in colonies, for example, sponges.

Phylum Coelenterata Tentacle-bearing animals with stinging cells.

Phylum Platyhelminthes Flatworms.

Phylum Annelida Segmented worms.

Phylum Mollusca Soft-bodied animals often with shells.

Phylum Arthropoda Jointed limbs; exoskeleton.

Phylum Echinodermata Spiny-skinned marine animals.

(b) ***VERTEBRATES*** (Phylum Chordata) Animals with a vertebrate column.

Class Mammalia (mammals) Hair; constant temperature; young suckled with milk.

SUMMARY

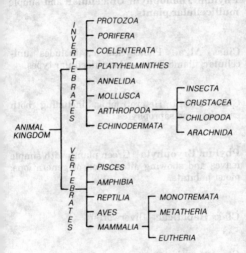

THE PLANT KINGDOM (major phyla)

Phylum Thallophyta Unicellular and simple **multicellular plants**.

Class Algae Photosynthetic; includes unicellular, filamentous, and multicellular types.

Class Fungi Heterotrophic; including both parasites and saprophytes.

Phylum Bryophyta Green plants with simple leaves and showing alternation of generations; moist habitats.

Class Hepaticae (liverworts)

Class Musci (mosses)

Phylum Pteridophyta (ferns; bracken; horsetails) Green plants, with roots, stems, leaves, and showing alternation of generations.

Phylum Spermatophyta Seed producing plants.

Class Gymnospermae Seeds produced in cones.

Class Angiospermae Flowering plants; seeds enclosed within fruits.

SUMMARY

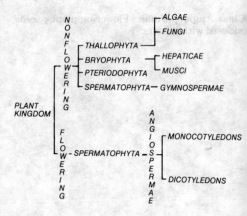

Bacteria and viruses do not meet the criteria necessary to be placed in either the animal or plant kingdoms.